P⸱

# EMERGENCY COMMUNICATIONS

# EMERGENCY COMMUNICATIONS

## LINDA K. MOORE

**Novinka Books**
*An imprint of Nova Science Publishers, Inc.*
New York

### NOTICE TO THE READER

**Library of Congress Cataloging-in-Publication Data:**
Moore, Linda K.
Emergency communications / Linda K. Moore.
   p. cm.
Includes index.
 ISBN 1-59454-888-9
 1. Public safety radio service. 2. Emergency communication systems--United States. 3. Internetworking (Telecommunication)--United States. 4. Radio frequency allocation--United States. I. Title.
TK6570.P8M66                                                        2006
363.34'7--dc22                                                 2005033099

*Published by Nova Science Publishers, Inc. New York*

# CONTENTS

# PREFACE

In evaluating the nation's emergency preparedness and response plans, Congress has reaffirmed its concern regarding the availability of spectrum to meet the wireless communications needs for public safety agencies. Many have voiced the need for a national plan for public safety telecommunications and spectrum management. This need is nested in the wider need for better policy and planning in spectrum management for all users and technologies.

Chapter One describes the Provisions of the Homeland Security Act of 2002 (P.L. 107-296) which instruct the Department of Homeland Security to address some of the issues concerning public safety communications. Several important policy decisions regarding spectrum use by first responders and other public safety organizations are under consideration by the Federal Communications Commission (FCC). The timely clearing of analog television broadcast channels intended for public safety use is the objective of H.R. 1425 (Harman). Provisions that could significantly impact emergency communications are included in S. 930, H.R. 1449, and H.R. 105, among others. Legislation that could impact the release of TV broadcast channels is proposed in H.R. 426. Future legislative initiatives in the 108th Congress could address the following areas:

**Interoperability.** The ability to communicate effectively among wireless networks used for public safety depends on spectrum use and compatible technology. In general the technology to support interoperability exists. For it to be fully implemented, three critical elements must be in place: standardization and coordination; comprehensive spectrum allocation; and funding.

**Spectrum Policy.** Sufficient and appropriate spectrum is fundamental to the future of wireless communications for public safety. The manner in which the spectrum is allocated is also important and this is illustrated, for example, in the problem of interference to public safety communications. This problem has opened a debate over how to reallocate spectrum not only to reduce interference but also to maximize benefit to other users in adjacent bands. Business and industrial users, for example, are examining their need for spectrum for applications in critical infrastructure security, such as pipeline surveillance.

**Technology.** The availability of new broadband technologies has further increased the need for spectrum. The FCC has recently allocated new spectrum for public safety broadband. The FCC has also allocated spectrum to test ultra-wideband (UWB) applications geared primarily to the needs of first responders.

This chapter focuses on key proposals for improving wireless telecommunications for public safety and recent actions to achieve this goal; the evolving role of the Department of Homeland Security is also discussed. The report will be updated and will be supplemented with shorter, topical reports.

In Chapter Two, the Emergency Alert System (EAS) is described as one of several federally managed warning systems. The Federal Emergency Management Agency (FEMA) jointly administers EAS with the Federal Communications Commission (FCC), in cooperation with the National Weather Service (NWS), an organization within the National Oceanic and Atmospheric Administration (NOAA). The NOAA/NWS weather radio system has been upgraded to an all-hazard warning capability. Ways to improve the NOAA network and the broader-based EAS are underway or are being tested. Much has been accomplished in recent years but the current hodgepodge of warning and alert systems is inadequate for fully alerting the public about terrorist attacks or natural disasters, or for providing information on how to respond. As was demonstrated on September 11, 2001, after the Southeast Asian tsunami on December 26, 2004, and again when Hurricane Katrina struck the Gulf Coast, the ability to communicate *after* a disaster also has a critical role in saving lives.

EAS is built on a structure conceived in the 1950's when over-the-air broadcasting was the best-available technology for widely disseminating emergency alerts. The Intelligence Reform and Terrorism Prevention Act (P.L. 108-458) has addressed the possibility of using advanced telecommunications and Internet technologies for emergency notification by requiring two projects for completion in 2005. Bills introduced in the 109th Congress that would improve emergency alert systems, domestically and internationally, include S. 50 (Senator Inouye) and H.R. 396 (Representative

Menendez). These bills were prompted by the tsunami disaster but include measures that also apply to the need for a better all-hazard warning system in the United States. Others — such as S. 34 (Senator Lieberman); S. 361 (Senator Snowe); S. 452 (Senator Corzine); H.R. 499 (Representative Shays); H.R. 882 (Representative Boehlert);H.R. 890 (Representative Pallone); H.R. 1584 (Representative Weldon); and H.R. 1674 (Representative Boehlert) — are concerned with tsunami detection and the initial stages of notification.

This chapter summarizes the technology and administration of EAS and the NOAA/NWS all-hazard network, and some of the key proposals for change. It will be updated.

# Chapter 1

# EMERGENCY COMMUNICATIONS: MEETING PUBLIC SAFETY SPECTRUM NEEDS

## INTRODUCTION

Heightened awareness of the integral role of the nation's wireless communications infrastructure in homeland security is bringing to the fore technical issues about public safety spectrum that have lain fallow for a number of years. This report covers issues concerning technology, the connection between technology standards and spectrum allocation, and the competition for spectrum among many users with diverse needs. The report in particular addresses two key issues that have attracted significant attention and controversy: interoperability and interference. Interoperability questions focus mainly on spectrum needs and compatible technology. Interference problems stem primarily from spectrum allocation decisions and radio-communications engineering that have combined to disrupt some public safety radio transmissions. Originally viewed by most industry stakeholders as separate topics, the two issues have, over time, coalesced into a single concern that questions different aspects of spectrum policy and technology planning.

This report has two main sections. In the first section "Identifying Public Safety Needs," some of the organizations involved with public safety telecommunications are introduced, and key activities dealing with wireless and spectrum issues are summarized. This section provides an overview of activity and government initiatives that have addressed wireless technology and spectrum use for public safety agencies. Some of the federal government functions have now been assigned to the Department of Homeland Security (DHS).

The second main section, "Spectrum for Public Safety," is organized by the major spectrum bands where public safety wireless communications are in use or planned. These are at: 100-512 MHz; 700 MHz; 800 MHz; 900 MHz and 4.9 GHz. Ultra-wide band (UWB) that broadcasts across a broad range of frequencies is also discussed. Recently, the Federal Communications Commission (FCC) proposed rules for public safety Dedicated Short-Range Communications Services (DSRC) in the 5.9 GHz band.[1] These services are embedded in Intelligent Transportation System (ITS) radio service.

The final section of this report recaps recent activities and legislation in the 107th and 108th Congresses regarding public safety and spectrum use.

# EMERGENCY COMMUNICATIONS ISSUES IN THE 108TH CONGRESS[2]

Congress may decide to take actions affecting public safety communications either with specific legislation for public safety needs or within the context of broader reforms of spectrum policy. If Congress passes legislation allocating additional spectrum for public safety, other spectrum planning policies may be impacted. Within the sphere of public safety, areas where Congress might be involved include funding and the reassignment of 700 MHz spectrum. Also, some public safety advocates have called for better coordination of interoperability programs, an area where Congress could assume leadership to consolidate and streamline the many federal government programs concerned with interoperability. Congressional actions concerning UWB could have an immediate impact on public safety.

Most wireless communications operate on designated frequencies using spectrum managed, in general, by either the Federal Communications Commission (FCC) or the National Telecommunications and Information Administration (NTIA). Among other responsibilities, the FCC supervises spectrum for services that include commercial wireless telephony, radio and television broadcasts, and non-federal public safety agency communications. The NTIA — part of the Department of Commerce — administers spectrum used by federal entities, and serves as the principal adviser to the executive branch on domestic and international telecommunications issues.

Congress may review the roles of the FCC and NTIA in implementing spectrum policy. The General Accounting Office (GAO) in a study released in late 2002,[3] were critical of FCC and NTIA spectrum management policies. Among its recommendations was a suggestion that the NTIA and FCC prepare reports for Congress on developing a national spectrum policy. The GAO report contends that the United States is lacking a cohesive policy, with negative consequences both domestically and in international negotiations. A follow-on report from the GAO, released in early 2003,[4] recommended the establishment of an independent commission to evaluate the need for spectrum management reform. Concurrently, the Department of Commerce has recommended that the NTIA be merged with the Department's Technology Administration within the International Trade Administration.[5] A related policy issue is the evaluation of the current division of responsibility in managing national spectrum policy, now conducted jointly by the FCC and NTIA. Legislative options include possible reform to the FCC and/or NTIA spectrum policy management. Or change may occur through modifications to the Department of Homeland Security which, at present, has no section that deals with spectrum.

During the second session of the 107th Congress, bipartisan support was rallied to forestall spectrum auctions by the Federal Communications Commission (FCC) that many believed would have jeopardized long-term planning for public safety spectrum use, both for improving interoperability and for eliminating interference. Shepherded through the House by members Dingell and Tauzin, the bill was introduced in the Senate in May, and compromise legislation became P.L. 107-195 on June 19, 2002. The intent of the bill is to protect spectrum in the 700 MHz band — where some frequencies have already been designated for public safety — while Congress reviews the spectrum auction process and considers legislation that might allocate additional spectrum in this band to public safety. The FCC must report to Congress not later than June 2003 on its actions in planning for the use of the affected frequencies.

Although varying in the specifics, there is consensus in, and considerable pressure from, the public safety sector to increase the amount of spectrum available in the 700 MHz band both to meet needs for growth and interoperability and to reduce interference in 800 MHz frequencies through relocation to 700 MHz frequencies. Congressmen Tauzin, Upton and Fossella contacted the FCC in July 2002 regarding interference in the 800 MHz frequencies. Resolution of the issues is clouded by requirements regarding the transition to digital television; as the law on the subject currently stands,[6] some frequencies in the 700 MHz range could be encumbered indefinitely. In the 108th Congress, policy makers may examine ways to ensure that first responders have adequate access to spectrum for emergency communications; also Congress may look at reforming the FCC to improve spectrum management and may also revisit legislation regarding the transition to digital television.[7] H.R. 1425, the "Homeland Emergency Response Operations Act," or the "HERO ACT," has the objective specifically to give the FCC the power to require immediate clearing of TV broadcast frequencies in the 700 MHz band that are designated for public safety.

In mid-2002, the Department of Commerce circulated draft legislation that proposed the creation of a Spectrum Relocation Fund. This would make it possible for federal agencies to cover relocation costs when they are required to vacate spectrum slated for commercial auction The Strom Thurmond National Defense Authorization Act of 1999 authorizes agencies to accept compensation payments when they relocate or modify frequency use in order to accommodate non-federal users. The Act further authorizes the NTIA and FCC to develop procedures for this. The NTIA has ruled that agencies must submit detailed estimates of costs. The FCC has suggested that these estimates be included in the auction process for the relevant spectrum; in effect, commercial bidders would be covering the costs of relocation. The Communications Act of 1934 must be modified to permit the agencies access to these funds. The 108th Congress has responded by introducing H.R. 1320 (Tauzin) and S. 865 (McCain), both called the Commercial Spectrum Enhancement Act, to create a Spectrum Relocation Fund.[8]

President Bush, in his Fiscal Year 2004 budget plan, emphasized the need for a spectrum transition fund. Other spectrum-related proposals in the budget are a request to Congress to provide enabling legislation for the FCC to levy user fees on unlicenced spectrum and to penalize broadcasters not vacating spectrum in the Upper 700 MHz band by the end of 2006.

To date, public policy has paid scant attention to the need for an integrated nationwide infrastructure for public safety communications. Various agency and committee efforts fall short of addressing the concept in its totality. Some concerns have been expressed regarding the fragmented nature of the public safety information and communications network. Experts decry the absence of a network overlay that assures end-to-end communications across the country. Concerns include the absence of redundancy in public safety networks and the lack of back-up locations for emergency communications.

A nationwide system might require linking DHS emergency notification functions, the Emergency Alert System, the nation's primary Public Safety Answering Points (about 5,500 emergency call centers, many of them locally operated and funded), other emergency call centers, mapping systems such as GIS,[9] and a plethora of local, state, tribal and federal emergency response centers. The complexity of such a network resembles that of the interlinked networks which support the nation's banking system. It would require similar levels of redundancy, back-up sites, and connectivity to critical databases and diagnostic systems; at the same time, it might encourage rationalization of operations and the elimination of some centers. It would also require close cooperation between the public and private sector under the administration of an agency with a focused portfolio of responsibilities, not unlike the Federal Reserve System.

Some industry observers have suggested that the FCC's policy-making functions be separated from the enforcement body; planning and oversight for public safety might be better administered through the NTIA. Whether as a division within NTIA or DHS, or as a separate agency, suggested oversight and planning functions would include: spectrum migration plans for the 800 MHz and 700 MHz bands; increased investment in developing new technology; improved development processes for standardization; a strategy for improved efficiency and digitization across networks; clarification of the role in public safety communications as part of critical infrastructure; consolidation of interoperability programs, with improved oversight; and, better coordination with similar agencies worldwide in the development of interoperability for first responders globally.

# BACKGROUND

Public safety agencies such as firefighters and police officers, and non-government organizations such as private ambulance services, are the nation's first responders in times of emergency. Communications, often wireless, are vital to these agencies' effectiveness and to the safety of their members and the public.

Redundancy and inter-connectivity are two key words in designing plans to protect critical telecommunications infrastructure. The catastrophic events at the World Trade Center and the Pentagon on September 11, 2001 provided many lessons in the successes and failures of telecommunications and information technology, particularly in responding to the massive crisis in lower Manhattan.

Despite major disruptions to wireline, wireless and broadcasting infrastructure, communications were sometimes gridlocked, but not paralyzed. Commercial cell phones were often useless because of insufficient capacity for the high demand, but telephones continued to function throughout most of the five boroughs of New York City. The Internet, built on packet-switch technology, operated normally and some of the survivors from the World Trade Center area found their way to safety guided by e-mail. The New York Stock Exchange shut down but the Federal Reserve System and the nation's banking network continued to function.[10] Priority access services established by the National Communications System were activated to assure that wireline phone calls among key federal personnel could move through busy telephone switches and that large-value payments over electronic networks were not disrupted. Telecommunications companies rushed additional equipment to the area and wherever possible switched connections from damaged switching centers to intact ones, even when operated by rival companies. Cell towers were rolled in to replace those lost in the holocaust. These were some of the successes.

At Ground Zero, turmoil predominated as first responders converged on the scene, arriving with incompatible communications equipment. Many perished in the twin towers because of inadequate communications, including the failure of outdated wireless communications equipment used by firefighters.[11]

In general, the systems that held up the best were those designed with redundancy and back-up in mind, where standardization and inter-modality are the norm. These systems, such as the banking system, relied on — and could often use interchangeably — internet, wireline and fiber optic communication backbones. They benefitted from significant investments in systems integration including seamless connectivity to operating systems and information databases. The systems that tended to fail were those with the least standardization, and sometimes with the least investment in needed technology. First responders' communications plans centered primarily on wireless technology and transmission over assigned bandwidths of spectrum; when the technologies and the radio frequencies didn't mesh, the back-up system was hand-carried notes. In addition to poor capacity for inter-connectivity — or interoperability — among public safety agencies, the wireless networks often lacked connections to databases and diagnostic systems.

Insufficient interoperability — the technical capacity of different systems to communicate with each other — is one of the defects in America's public safety communications networks. Interoperability is indicative of the problems besetting these networks. Common factors interoperability shares with other components of the country's flawed public safety communications infrastructure include:

- *Unresolved questions regarding spectrum*: amount needed, bandwidth locations and regulations for use.
- *Incomplete standards*: rooted in a long history of proprietary manufacturer standards that stocked public safety agencies with incompatible hardware.
- *Lagging technology*: throughout the country, public safety agencies at the local, state and federal level are using technology that many studies have described as outmoded. New communications technologies exist but are barely implemented for a variety of reasons relating to cost, organization and the technical capabilities of various public safety agencies.
- *Lack of a coordinating network policy*: exemplified by an absence of operational standards or protocols and incomplete efforts for federal/state/local programs for cooperation and coordination.

## SPECTRUM

Radio frequency spectrum provides an invisible roadway for wireless transmissions; each band of measured spectrum is like a highway lane guiding communications to their destination. It is used for all forms of wireless communications, such as cellular telephony, paging, radio and television broadcast, telephone radio relay, aeronautical and maritime radio navigation, and satellite command and control. Users include federal, state, local and tribal governments, private industry, and amateur radio operators. Commercial operators include broadcasters, wireless communications companies, and the manufacturing, transportation and utilities industries. Government users include agencies of the federal government and state and local public safety agencies. Spectrum, a valuable resource, limited by technology, is managed by the federal government to maximize efficiency in its use and to prevent interference among spectrum users.

Wireless (radio frequency) spectrum is measured in cycles per second, or hertz (Hz).[12] Spectrum allocations are divided into channels. Placing many channels in a designated spectrum band constitutes narrowband. Broadband has comparatively fewer channels and therefore greater capacity for sending images and other data at high speeds. Contiguous spectrum for broadband is important for advanced wireless applications.

The term wideband is sometimes used in the telecommunications industry to describe limited broadband applications transmitted on narrowband channels. An example is "mobile data" for public safety. This provides voice and data communications and supports interoperability for text messages.

Currently, non-federal public safety agency communications use VHF and UHF[13] frequencies below 512 MHz and UHF frequencies in the 806-824/851-869 MHz ranges.[14] At 4.9 GHz, the FCC has recently designated 50 MHz for public safety. Also, ultra-wideband technology that has been provisionally approved will be used for public safety. The trends in public safety technology and spectrum management are on track to place broadband in higher frequencies and to develop digital narrowband and wideband in the lower frequencies. The lower bands (illustrated below) are the main focus of discussions about spectrum policy and management. (Note that spectrum at 764-776/794-806 MHz, designated in the illustration with an asterisk, is not yet available for use by public safety.)

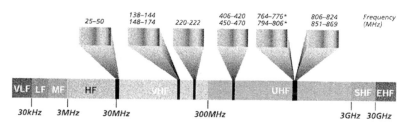

Source: Public Safety Wireless Communications Systems, PSWN Program Information Brief

Figure 1. Public Safety Spectrum Bands

Because public safety networks operate on many different frequencies and because most wireless communications equipment in use has been designed to operate on a limited number of frequencies, interoperability is a critical technical issue. Interoperability means that different public safety agency networks can readily contact each other in a mission-critical situation because they have invested in the necessary communications technology and infrastructure. In general the technology to support interoperability exists. For it to be fully implemented, three critical elements must be in place:

standardization and coordination; comprehensive spectrum allocation; and funding.

# IDENTIFYING PUBLIC SAFETY NEEDS

There are a number of programs that deal with public safety communications and spectrum — the product of two decades of efforts to build consensus, establish national goals and priorities, identify technical issues, and implement programs. Each program mentioned below and others not discussed in this report (including several that are defunct) has contributed to the development of information and expertise that provide an invaluable resource for public safety communications planners. There are many entities that have contributed and continue to contribute to the furtherance of public safety spectrum programs. Some would say that there are too many federal initiatives, however, and that consolidation is needed. This section summarizes some of the efforts by agencies and associations. For federal entities, reallocation of responsibility under the Department of Homeland Security is also referenced.

## National Communications System

The National Communications System (NCS) was established at the Department of Defense by Executive Order in 1984 "to assist the President, the National Security Council, the Director of the Office of Science and Technology Policy and the Director of the Office of Management and Budget in: (1) the exercise of the telecommunications functions and responsibilities, and (2) the coordination of the planning for and provision of national security and emergency preparedness communications. . ." It consults with the National Security Telecommunications Advisory Committee (NSTAC), among others, on issues related to national security and emergency preparedness telecommunications. It is closely linked to the White House through NSTAC, which advises the President on national security telecommunications matters, and the National Security Council.

Now part of DHS (Title II), the National Communications System is comprised of 23 federal agencies.[15] NCS worked with the telecommunications industry to create the wireline priority access system and is moving forward with the development of a nationwide wireless priority service. NCS divisions include: Critical Infrastructure Protection, Plans and Resources, and Technology and Programs. The primary focus of its programs is to support inter-connectivity of federal agency communications at all times and to assure communications links in times of crisis. Although wireless communications can use frequencies allocated to government agencies, most wireline (landline) communications are supplied by national carriers. Therefore, close cooperation with the telecommunications industry is among NCS's responsibilities.

NCS activities include participation in several multi-agency and public-private sector endeavors. These are:

- Advanced Intelligent Network (AIN) Program
  - National Coordinating Center (NCC)
- Alerting and Coordination Network (ACN)
- SHAred RESources (SHARES) Project Office
  - SHARES HF Interoperability Working Group
- Training, Planning and Operational Support (TOPS)
  - Office of Priority Telecommunications
  - Telecommunications Service Priority (TSP)
- Technology and Programs Division
- Government Emergency Telecommunications Service (GETS)
  - Wireless Priority Service (WPS)

Newer programs that are expected to gain momentum under the direction of NCS deal with interoperability and Wireless Priority Service (WPS). Interoperability is the capacity to communicate with different administrative structures using different technologies and requires — among other things — common technical standards and protocols, appropriate interface technologies and, for wireless communications, compatible spectrum allocations. Under the current NCS structure, the two programs most involved with advancing interoperability are the SHARES Project Office — focused on developing technology — and the Technology and Programs Division — which manages GETS and WPS and also addresses standards.

SHARES are charged with promoting interoperability primarily through the SHARES HF Interoperability Working Group. The objective of the group is to develop HF (High Frequency) radio in combination with other communications technologies such as satellite and VHF/UHF radio (the standard for most public safety agency communications). Improved technology that makes HF radio widely accessible provides benefits such as improved spectrum efficiency and high-speed image transmission.

Wireless Priority Service is an outgrowth of GETS, the program that ensures priority access service to telephone lines for federal national security and emergency preparedness users in times of emergency. The WPS initiative dates to the period immediately following the attacks of September 11, 2001, when cell phone activity was disrupted by high demand. WPS has been operational in New York City and Washington since May 2002 and is expanding to other metropolitan areas. According to Breton C. Greene, Deputy Manager of NCS, it is hoped that WPS will be operational nationwide by the end of 2003. WPS will be provided through commercial wireless carriers that have signed or will sign contracts with NCS through DynCorp, a private company, designated as a Government Emergency Telecommunications and Wireless Priority integration contractor.[16] NCS also plans to reach out to state and local authorities to encourage their participation in GETS.[17]

## Public Safety Wireless Advisory Committee

The Public Safety Wireless Advisory Committee (PSWAC) was chartered in 1995, at the request of Congress, to study public safety spectrum and make recommendations for meeting spectrum needs through the year 2010. The following year, PSWAC submitted a report[18] containing recommendations for the improvement of public safety communications over wireless networks. Key among these was the request for 95 MHz of additional spectrum for state and local public safety needs. The report concluded that current federal public safety spectrum bands would meet projected requirements through 2010, providing there were no interim reductions in the amount allocated. In response to this report, Congress directed the FCC to allocate 24 MHz of spectrum to non-federal public safety agencies from the 746-806 MHz range as part of the reallocation of channels 60-69, to be cleared in the migration from analog to digital television broadcasting.[19]

## Federal Law Enforcement Wireless Users Group

Several interagency groups were established to address public safety wireless issues following the National Performance Review (NPR) issued by

Vice President Gore in 1993. The NPR called for, among other things, the nationwide development of interoperable wireless systems for all types of public safety agencies at the local, state, and federal levels of government. As a result, in 1994, a Memorandum of Understanding between the Departments of Justice and the Treasury formalized what had been an ad hoc working group as the Federal Law Enforcement Wireless Users Group (FLEWUG). Its role is to assist federal agencies in sharing information about wireless communications issues and to "plan, coordinate and implement future shared-use wireless telecommunications systems and resources."[20] among its goals are the development of common standards for land mobile radio, improving interoperability, and identifying cost-saving processes. More than 30 federal departments and agencies are members of the users group.

## Public Safety Wireless Network (PSWN Program)

FLEWUG created the Public Safety Wireless Network (PSWN) Program[21] in 1996 to implement plans to foster interoperability among wireless networks. The PSWN Program explores options available for providing spectrally efficient, interoperable, and cost-effective wireless communications that will meet the requirements of local, state, and federal public safety organizations. It provides consultative services to states and tribal nations in matters such as developing interoperability programs, strategic planning, spectrum management, and identifying funding sources. PSWN is jointly financed through the Departments of Justice and Treasury.

Shortly after September 11, 2001, PSWN petitioned the FCC to revisit the need for additional spectrum for wireless communications within and between public safety agencies and other first responders.[22] In the report it filed with the FCC, PSWN noted that spectrum from channels 60-69 (the Upper 700 MHz band) designated for public safety use by the FCC had still not been freed for this purpose. It reiterated the need for spectrum to support interoperability and made recommendations for additional allocations for public safety communications that would meet the spectrum needs identified by PSWAC in 1996. Specifically, PSWN identified the need for more spectrum for interoperability below 512 MHz and requested that spectrum in the 4.9 GHz range be used for public safety instead of being auctioned for commercial use. The report evoked the potential for using this spectrum for numerous broadband applications and new technologies that would aid first responders. The 24 MHz in the Upper 700 MHz band is judged by PSWN and others[23] to be insufficient for broadband. Also they believe additional spectrum is needed for localized network support such as Personal Area Network/Vehicular Area Network (PAN/VAN) systems.

PSWN subsequently prepared analyses of the effectiveness of communications in the New York and Washington, D.C. metropolitan areas after the attacks of September 11. The reports evaluate the level of interoperability among the public safety agencies responding to the attacks as well as other measures of performance. Some of the recommendations developed as a result of the studies cover specific steps that could be implemented by public safety agencies at all levels to enhance communications interoperability.

In 1998, PSWN estimated the total cost to replace existing core infrastructure for public safety telecommunications systems nationwide at $18.3 billion.[24] The costs for upgrading systems with new technologies, additional features, and interoperable capabilities would be higher.

## Project SAFECOM

Authorized by the Office of Management and Budget (OMB) as one of 24 electronic government (e-government)[25] initiatives, the primary objective of this program is to support interoperability. Responsibility for the Wireless Public SAFEty Interoperable COMmunications Program, dubbed Project SAFECOM, had been assigned by the OMB to the Wireless Directorate of the Department of the Treasury. At the recommendation of the Chief Information Officers of several federal agencies, including the Departments of Treasury, Commerce and Justice, Project SAFECOM was transferred to FEMA and followed that agency to the Department of Homeland Security.[26] DHS has now assumed the role of managing partner. In line with a department-wide policy to have all technology prototype projects headed by the one directorate, the development stage of SAFECOM will be managed by the Science and Technology Directorate.[27]

Before its transfer to DHS, SAFECOM managers had been working closely with PSWN on outreach programs, primarily to states. Although, long-term, SAFECOM had expected to facilitate "convergent integration" to develop a unified national system for public safety communications, short-term goals included identifying interoperability solutions that could be funded through existing grants programs. Because of the inter-relationship between technology and spectrum, SAFECOM's unofficial position on spectrum policy was that final decisions on spectrum allocation should not be made until requirements documents established specific needs for bandwidth. In the opinion of Steve Cooper, Chief Information Officer for DHS, SAFECOM " has not produced any useable results" and that an "entirely different approach" is needed.[28] The long-term objectives of Project SAFECOM are to achieve, nationwide: federal-to-federal interoperability; federal-to-state/local interoperability; and state/local interoperability.

## The Federal Communications Commission

The FCC has created several key administrative groups to participate in spectrum management and planning. In 1986, it formed the National Public Safety Planning Advisory Committee to advise it on management of spectrum in the 800 MHZ band, newly designated for public safety. The following year, the FCC adopted a Public Safety National Plan that, among other things, established Regional Planning Committees (RPCs) to develop plans that met specific planning needs. The regional planning approach is also being applied to spectrum in the Upper 700 MHz band.[29] The FCC encourages the formation of RPCs with a broad base of participation. The RPCs have flexibility in determining how best to meet state and local needs, including spectrum use and technology.

### *Public Safety National Coordinating Committee*

Technical and operational standards for the Upper 700 MHz band are developed and recommended to the FCC through the Public Safety National Coordination Committee (NCC). Established by the FCC in 1999, the NCC has a Steering Committee of government, the public safety community, and the telecommunications equipment manufacturing industry. Government agencies that are co-sponsors of the NCC, with the FCC, are the NTIA, FEMA, and the Departments of Justice and the Treasury. NCC is also working on a plan for nationwide interoperability. The NCC is submitting recommendations to the FCC for broadband technology on these public safety bandwidths. Standards for other public safety technologies using 700 MHz have

been established and the technical specifications have been agreed upon and sent to manufacturers. Issues of coordination that must still be agreed upon include channel-naming protocols. The FCC has declined to rule on naming protocols, saying the industry should reach consensus according to "best practices," and not by mandate.[30] The charter for the NCC is scheduled to expire in 2003.

## FCC and Homeland Security

The Homeland Security Policy Council (HSPC), formed by the FCC in November 2001, has announced initiatives "to improve public safety by addressing spectrum issues, including interoperability and redundancy."[31] To this end, the HSPC is providing coordination and oversight of the FCC's actions related to public safety, many of which are discussed in this report. The HSPC is comprised of FCC staff; all divisions are represented. Its proposed role is to work closely with federal departments and agencies, notably the NCS, in coordinating "interagency and industry partnerships; infrastructure protection; communications reliability; public safety communications; spectrum policy; new technologies."[32]

In January, 2002, HSPC rechartered the Network Reliability and Interoperability Council (NRIC). The role of NRIC is to develop recommendations for the FCC and the telecommunications industry to insure optimal reliability, interoperability, and inter-connectivity of public telecommunications networks and the Internet. The Council's members are senior representatives from the telecommunications industry.[33] Richard C. Notebaert, Chairman and Chief Executive Officer of Qwest Communications is Council Chairman. NRIC created focus groups to identify issues and make recommendations. The Homeland Security Public Safety Group has submitted its report, identifying commercial communications services presently used by Public Safety, with recommendations for "best practices" by private industry.[34]

Later in 2002, HSPC chartered the Media Security and Reliability Council as a Federal Advisory Committee for a two-year period.[35] The Committee is comprised primarily of senior executives (*e.g.* President, Chief Executive Officer) from broadcasting, satellite and cable companies. In May 2003, the Council received recommendations for best practices in emergency communications, including all-hazard warnings and the Emergency Alert System.[36]

## Spectrum Policy Task Force

A cross-bureau, multi-disciplinary task force was announced June 6, 2002 to assist the FCC in identifying and evaluating changes in spectrum policy. Comprised of senior staff from within the FCC, the Task Force sought public comment on spectrum policy. Additionally, workshops were scheduled during July and August 2002 to facilitate debate on policy topics. In the request for comments, the FCC provided five major categories of policy issues: (1) market-oriented allocation and assignment; (2) interference protection; (3) spectral efficiency; (4) public safety communications; (5) international issues.

Four working groups were created to organize the information collected: Interference Protection; Spectrum Efficiency; Spectrum Rights and Responsibilities; and Unlicenced and Experimental. Public safety spectrum issues and recommendations were subsumed by the working groups. Discussions of interference, for example, focused on common technical problems and possible solutions but did not specifically address interference problems experienced on frequencies used by public safety.

On November 15, 2002, the Task Force released a report containing its findings and recommendations.[37] The FCC's request for comments on this report extended into February2003.[38] In keeping with recent FCC policy announcements, the Task Force favored market-driven solutions. It identified three general models for assigning spectrum usage rights. These are: "exclusive use" — industry-friendly, flexible licensing agreements; "commons" — shared frequencies used by an unlimited number of unlicenced users; and "command and control" — the "traditional" approach to spectrum management by the FCC, where uses are limited by regulation.

In discussing the model appropriate for managing public safety spectrum, the Task Force suggested that "command and control" should remain to ensure essential services but more flexibility in sharing or leasing spectrum capacity should be allowed. In particular, the Task Force recommended that public safety agencies should be allowed to rent frequencies to commercial users on a secondary basis, recovering the capacity in time of crisis. One of the characteristics of spectrum demand for public safety uses is heavy peak demand and low average use. In the Legislative Recommendations that conclude the study, the Task Force suggested that Congress initiate a review of the potential use of spectrum fees for non-market based spectrum uses (including public safety). A model for this approach could be a recently-implemented British spectrum policy that charges public service for use of spectrum utilizing a formula related to commercial values for spectrum use. The objective is to make public agencies more efficient in their use of spectrum. PSWN was among those filing objections to the proposal for a fee schedule for public safety users.[39]

# National Telecommunications and Information Administration

To address the need for interoperability spectrum, in June 1999 the NTIA designated certain federally-allocated radio frequencies for use by federal, state, and local law enforcement and incident response entities. The frequencies are from exclusive federal spectrum, and are adjacent to spectrum used by state and local governments. NTIA's "interoperability plan," developed in coordination with the Interdepartmental Radio Advisory Committee (IRAC)[40] and the Federal Law Enforcement Wireless Users Group, was intended to improve communications in response to emergencies and threats to public safety. NTIA described the plan, along with the efforts of the FCC and PSWN, as one of "the first steps to ensuring that sufficient radio spectrum is available when and where an emergency or public safety need may arise."

The NTIA created a Public Safety Program Office in 1996 to coordinate federal government activities for spectrum and telecommunications relating to public safety. In June 2002, the Public Safety Program and PSWN co-sponsored an "executive leadership summit" on public safety interoperability. Speakers from public and private sectors presented viewpoints regarding interoperability, partnerships, funding and new technology.[41]

Within the Department of Commerce, NTIA has been responsible for the Critical Infrastructure Assurance Program for information and Communications. This function has been transferred to the DHS Directorate for Information Analysis and Infrastructure Protection (Title II). The Department of Commerce has recommended that the NTIA be merged with the Department's Technology Administration within the International Trade Administration.[42]

# Department of Defense Spectrum Management

The focal point for public safety spectrum management within the Department of Defense has been the Office of Spectrum Analysis and Management (OSAM), created in 1998. As part of a reorganization that will provide more resources for spectrum management, OSAM will be subsumed by a new Defense Spectrum Office.[43] Among its functions are to provide strategic planning for spectrum management, analyze the impact of sharing spectrum on current and future military operations, coordinate the development and implementation of spectrum management technologies, and ensure the efficient use of spectrum. Early in 2002, a new senior post was created at the Pentagon for spectrum management: deputy assistant secretary of Defense for spectrum and C3 (command, control, and communications) policy.

## Federal Emergency Management Agency

The Office of National Preparedness at FEMA was chartered by President Bush in May 2001 to coordinate federal programs at the Departments of Defense, Justice, Health and Human Services, and Energy focused on "weapons of mass destruction consequence management." The Office of National Preparedness (ONP) was comprised of the affected agencies, plus the Coast Guard, the U.S. Fire Administration and representatives of local first responders, among others. Post 9-11, the Office of Homeland Security asked the new FEMA office to study the response capability at the state level in case of terrorist attack. Prior to the creation of a Department of Homeland Security, the ONP had begun to structure a program to assist first responders, centered on key steps such as training, joint exercises, national assessment, and grants for training and equipment. FEMA activities are being consolidated and continued under the Emergency Preparedness and Response Directorate (EPR) of DHS (Title V).[44] Anti-terrorist functions at ONP, however, were transferred to the Office of Domestic Preparedness (ODP), administered by the Directorate of Border and Transportation Security (Title IV). The ODP had previously been part of the Office of Justice programs (see below). Several bills before Congress (notably S. 930 and H.R. 105) call for the restoration of the Office of National Preparedness, to be managed by FEMA within DHS.

### *Emergency Alert System and "Reverse 911"*

FEMA provides direction for state and local emergency officials in planning and implementing emergency alerts using the Emergency Alert System (EAS).[45] EAS went live in 1997 as the digitized replacement of the Emergency Broadcast System. It broadcasts warnings over radio, television and most cable channels. EAS was designed by the FCC and is jointly managed by the FCC and FEMA, in cooperation with the National Weather Service of the National Oceanic and Atmospheric Administration (NOAA). Historically, the bulk of emergency alerts broadcast over the EAS system have been weather-related natural disasters. Originally conceived during the

Truman administration, what is now known as EAS was to be used to alert the populace in case of a threat to the nation, such as a nuclear attack. In 1963, the emergency alert system was extended to state and local communities. Broadcast stations are required to disseminate emergency messages from the president; cooperation at the state and local level is optional. The national alert system has never been used by a president.

EAS was not activated at either the national or local level on September 11 and this episode in the history of EAS brought the validity of the system into question by many. In particular, the question has been raised as to whether a broadcast system is the best way to alert people in time-critical emergencies. Among the proposals addressing this concern is one for the development of warning systems that use existing technology for 911 calls to provide telephone subscribers with a telephone warning of an emergency system — commonly referred to as "reverse 911." This technology could be extended to cell phone subscribers and users of various messaging devices based on Internet or other communications protocols.[46]

## Department of Justice

The Office for Domestic Preparedness (ODP) at the Office of Justice Programs and related functions of the Attorney General have been transferred to the Directorate of Border and Transportation Security(Title IV).[47] ODP grant programs that include telecommunications for first responders, administered by the domestic preparedness office, will reportedly be coordinated with grant programs from other incorporated agencies, notably FEMA (Emergency Preparedness and Response, Title V).

The ODP (formerly the Office for State and Local Domestic Preparedness) was created by the Attorney General after Congress expressed concern about state readiness to respond to chemical or biological attacks. In 1998, funds were authorized for equipment and training for state and local public safety personnel to respond to and manage terrorist incidents involving weapons of mass destruction.[48]

States are eligible to receive ODP grants if they have filed a plan for Domestic Preparedness. Funds for equipment are available through a standardized equipment program that provides a menu of approved categories. These categories include personal protection equipment, detection equipment, decontamination equipment, and communications equipment. For the most part, operational capabilities and performance standards are not specified within categories of equipment.

Justice also administers two major assistance grant programs centered on law enforcement. These are the Byrne Formula Grant Program[49] and the Local Law Enforcement Block Grants (LLEBG) Program.[50] The LLEBG Program grants are made directly to local government agencies or in block grants to states that then distribute the funds. Procuring equipment, technology and other material directly related to basic law enforcement is one of the purposes eligible for grants and this can be used for telecommunications. The Byrne Formula Grants do not cover public safety communications. These two programs will remain with the Bureau of Justice Assistance.

The functions of the Office of Science and Technology at National Institute of Justice (NIJ) and of NIJ itself have been reestablished, modified and expanded by the Homeland Security Act of 2002.[51] Under the new law, the Office of Science and Technology is under the authority of the Assistant Attorney General, Office of Justice Programs, within the National Institute of Justice.

In 1998, NIJ created the AGILE Program to combine all interoperability projects then underway at NIJ.[52] The program addresses interim and long-term interoperability solutions through standardization encompassing wireless telecommunications and information technology applications. The AGILE Program also has provided funding to Regional Planning Committees for start-up costs and the preparation and distribution of regional plans. The focus of AGILE has been on interoperability within criminal justice agencies and between public safety agencies. The National Institute of Justice has managed the Justice Technology Information Network as part of the Office of Science and Technology. Prior to the creation of the Department of Homeland Security, it had been proposed that this and related programs at Justice be integrated with project SAFECOM.

In an effort to develop cooperation for interoperability at all levels of government, AGILE has taken an active role in the formation of the National Task Force on Interoperability (NTFI).[53] Task Force discussions on how to address interoperability in a more comprehensive way led to the creation and distribution of guidelines to public officials. The purpose of these guidelines is to raise awareness about the importance of interoperability, its impact on constituents, steps needed to prepare for interoperability and other issues.

## Department of Homeland Security

Provisions of the Homeland Security Act of 2002 (P.L. 107-296) instruct the Department of Homeland Security (DHS) to address some of the issues concerning public safety communications in emergency preparedness and response and in providing critical infrastructure. Telecommunications for first responders is mentioned in several sections, with specific emphasis on technology for interoperability. National strategy for homeland security requires investments in technology to improve response time and decision-making in detecting and responding to potential or actual threats. DHS potentially can expand that strategy to include state, regional, local and tribal communications resources. The Act does specify support for improving interoperability for first responders. Interoperability refers to the ability of different communications systems, especially radio-based networks, to connect with each other. Until recently, many first responders have not given much attention to communications equipment compatibility. To achieve interoperability in the field requires radio equipment that operates on new frequencies as well as coordination in areas such as operational protocols, command center management, and spectrum use.

Title I of the Homeland Security Act creates the executive Department and the position of Chief Information Officer.[54] The Chief Information Office is responsible for coordinating information sharing nationwide and for meeting other communications needs within DHS, throughout the federal government, and for state and local first responders. Title II, dealing with Information Analysis and Infrastructure Protection (IAIP), establishes an Office of Science and Technology within the directorate. Duties include research and development support for law enforcement agencies for "wire and wireless interoperable communications technologies."[55] The National Communications System is responsible for telecommunications under the Secretariate of Information Analysis and Infrastructure Protection.[56] A Homeland Security Advisory System is created within IAIP[57] to provide warning information in coordination with other federal agencies.

The responsibilities of Managing Partner for Project SAFECOM will be assumed by the Science and Technology Directorate. Responsibilities of Emergency Preparedness and Response cover "comprehensive programs for developing interoperative communications technology, and helping to ensure that emergency response providers acquire such technology."[58] These departmental obligations conceivably can encompass all matters related to public safety communications since, arguably, all new systems should be "interoperable." Border and Transportation Security functions include grant programs from the Office of Domestic Preparedness, discussed below.

## Federal Response Plan

The Federal Response Plan was initially developed by FEMA in conjunction with 26 other federal departments or agencies and is now under the supervision of the DHS Emergency Preparedness and Response directorate.[59] The Department of Homeland Security is the lead agency for the Federal Response Plan, a detailed plan of lines of responsibility and appropriate actions for response and recovery. There are a dozen Emergency Support Function Annexes, including communications, each with a designated primary agency and support agencies. DHS is the primary agency for the Communications annex; designated support agencies include the Department of Agriculture, Forest Service; Department of Commerce; Department of Defense; Department of the Interior; Federal Communications Commission; and the General Services Administration. The designated departments have responsibility for various aspects of emergency communications and network infrastructure.

## Coordination of Emergency Communications Activities

Within DHS, several separate initiatives exist that support emergency communications, especially as regards interoperability for first responders. As noted above, within IAIP both the NCS and Project SAFECOM support interoperability programs. Two other DHS directorates have funding and leadership roles that are generally viewed to have an impact on the deployment of interoperability projects at the state and local level. Federal departments and agencies with interoperability projects include several that are participants in emergency communications operations within the Federal Response Plan. Federal programs to foster interoperability with significant involvement at the state and local level include: National Task Force for Interoperability(Department of Justice); PSWN Program (Departments of Justice and Treasury); Public Safety Planning Office (NTIA); and Public Safety National Coordinating Committee and Network Reliability and Interoperability Committee (FCC). Additionally, the FCC and NTIA implement spectrum policy, including frequency allocations and management for federal and state and local first responders.

A report released by the Republican Main Street Partnership[60] has advocated the participation of DHS in spectrum negotiations on a footing similar to that already accorded DOD and other federal agencies. The report noted the importance of spectrum because it is integral to the communications of homeland security response. It stressed the need to "review and establish a clear picture of the frequency spectrum needs of the Department" and other agencies, including state and local agencies, with which it will be operating.

## Other Organizations

Many other associations and government agencies work actively to solve critical issues concerning public safety spectrum. The Association of Public-Safety Communications Officials, International (APCO),[61] for example, has taken a leadership role in dealing with problems of network interference and interoperability. APCO is a charter member of the National Public Safety Telecommunications Council (NPSTC),[62] a federation of associations. The Council was created in 1997 to follow up on recommendations made by the Public Safety Wireless Advisory Committee. In addition, the group acts as a resource and advocate for public safety telecommunications issues. Other charter members include FEMA, International Association of Emergency Managers, National Association of State Telecommunications Directors, National Association of State Emergency Medical Services Directors, American Association of State Highway Transportation Officials, and the International Association of Fire Chiefs.

## SPECTRUM FOR PUBLIC SAFETY

Congestion, interoperability, interference, access, and sufficient spectrum to support broadband technologies communications are the major concerns most often mentioned in discussions of public safety wireless communications. The following review of public safety spectrum discusses different bands in reference to what appears to be the dominant topic of debate regarding that frequency.

## Congestion: 100-512 MHz Range

The need for spectrum for interoperability is particularly acute in the lower spectrum ranges, where the majority of agencies operate. FCC licensing records show that the frequencies between 150-174 MHz are the most intensively used. Surveys by PSWN and others indicate that approximately 73% of all law enforcement entities and 65% to 70% of firefighters and EMS agencies operate land-mobile radio systems in the 100-300 MHz bands, the VHF high-band.[63] Out-dated analog equipment adds to this congestion; the cost of acquiring spectrum-efficient narrowband technology has delayed plans for conversion.

To facilitate interoperability and ease congestion in public safety channels below 512MHz, Congress as part of appropriations for 2001, reclaimed for federal use 3MHz of spectrum that had previously been designated for mixed use in the 138-144 MHz band.[64] The Act also requested studies on spectrum use and reallocation from the DOD, NTIA and FCC. The DOD was required to study the 138-144 MHz band — which it occupies — for possible sharing with public safety. The NTIA and the FCC were required to jointly submit a report to Congress on alternative frequencies available for public safety.

The NTIA responded by identifying bands used by public safety and by the federal government between 100 MHz and 1000 MHz.[65] It defined alternative frequencies as spectrum comparable to 138-144 MHz and concluded that the 162-174 MHz and 406.1- 420 MHz bands met the criteria for comparable spectrum. After a detailed examination of the federal uses of these bands, the NTIA concluded that new sharing with non-federal public safety agencies was not feasible. It noted the federal government has a policy in effect that designates 40 channels for nationwide interoperability between federal, state and local public safety entities within the bands the NTIA studied. These channels encompass 0.5 MHz of spectrum. The NTIA report further noted that first PSWAC and then PSWN had recommended a minimum of 2.5 MHz be set aside for interoperability.

In identifying non-federal government spectrum as alternatives to the 138-144 MHz band, the FCC focused primarily on VHF frequencies administered under its authority because it deemed VHF to be "most comparable" to the 138-144 MHz band. Noting that some channels in the VHF high-band have been designated for interoperability, the FCC focused on identifying frequencies that would be close to those already in use in order to support broadband radio. Broadband technology is more efficient when contiguous or nearly contiguous channels are used. After reviewing current uses in comparable frequencies, the FCC concluded that reallocation would excessively disrupt incumbent users.[66]

Neither the NTIA nor the FCC recommended spectrum in the studied ranges that could be reallocated for exclusive public safety use. The DOD, in a classified document, reportedly concluded that sharing could be possible in the 138-144 MHz band if evaluated on a case-by-case basis.[67]

## Interoperability: Upper 700 MHz Band

For administrative purposes, the FCC refers to the 700 MHz Band as the "Lower 700" (channels 52-59) and the "Upper 700" (channels 60-69).[68] Public safety uses are allocated for the Upper 700 MHz band. Due mainly to the combination of different technology standards operating on different radio frequencies, communications between — and even within — local, state and federal agencies are not always assured. Achieving interoperability is an important goal of the public safety community. In the last decade, significant advances in technology and in funding to purchase communications equipment have eased, but not eliminated, problems of incompatible systems, inadequate technology, insufficient funding, and limited spectrum.

### Analog TV: Channels 60-69

Congress passed legislation[69] in 1997 with the intention of assuring an orderly and equitable transition from analog to digital television broadcasting. As mandated by Congress, analog television broadcasts on all channels, including 60-69, were to be phased out and the cleared spectrum reallocated for wireless communications. Following the instructions of Congress, the FCC assigned the frequencies 764-776 MHz and 794-806 MHz, in channels 63-64 and 68-69 respectively, for public safety use. At the behest of many public safety organizations, the FCC designated 2.5 MHz of this allocation specifically for interoperability. Channels 60-62[70] and 65-67[71] were identified for auction for commercial wireless use.

Congress set a date of December 31, 2006 for the cessation of analog television operations on channels 60-69, instructing the FCC to restrict broadcast licensing accordingly. At the same time, Congress required that the FCC grant exemptions for an undefined period of time if three major conditions were met. Briefly, these conditions are: 1) if one or more of the television stations affiliated with the four national networks are not broadcasting a DTV signal, 2) if digital to analog converter technology is not generally available in the market of the licensee, or 3) — often referred to as the "15% rule" — if at least 15% of the television households in the market served by the station do not subscribe to a digital "multi-channel video programming distributor" (including cable or satellite services) and do not have DTV sets or converters.[72]

Standards for narrowband radio applications in the Upper 700 MHz were recommended by the National Coordinating Committee to the FCC and adopted in early 2001. The NCC is also responsible for developing standards for wideband, particularly interoperable wideband. Standardization is essential for interoperability. Manufacturers that specialize in public safety telecommunications are testing new wideband applications but they will not produce equipment to operate at 700 MHz in quantity until the standards have been finalized through the FCC and the market for the equipment has been scoped. The size of the potential market is prescribed by the availability of spectrum.

In some localities, the needed Upper 700 MHz spectrum is already unencumbered. For the most part, however, the band has not been cleared and is still occupied by television broadcasting. Recognizing that this spectrum is encumbered, Tom Sugrue, then Chief of the FCC's Wireless Telecommunications Bureau has said, "many in the public safety community, and in the broadcast community, and in the commercial wireless industry, believe that if the statute remains in its present form, there will be very few stations that actually vacate the 700 MHz band by 2006."[73]

### *Voluntary Clearing, Auctions and User Fees*

Among the provisions concerning digital TV is the requirement that spectrum in channels 60-69 not turned over to public safety agencies be auctioned for commercial purposes. The mandated auction was originally scheduled for May 2000, but was postponed repeatedly. The FCC worked with the broadcasting industry and wireless carriers on a "market-driven" approach for voluntary clearing of the spectrum to be auctioned or assigned to public safety agencies.[74]

Any initiative that expedites band clearing for auctioned spectrum may concurrently free up encumbered spectrum for public safety agencies. In some situations, stringent FCC rules regarding interference will require the vacating of adjacent public safety spectrum. An example of band clearing, cited by the FCC, would be for a wireless telecommunications company acquiring spectrum (for commercial use) in channel 67 in a major metropolitan area. An analog television station transmitting on channel 68 (designated for public safety) in the same area would also have to be cleared to meet FCC rules regarding interference. For the same reason, the FCC decided to include channel 59 in its band clearing and reallocation efforts for the Upper 700 MHz band because this channel must also be cleared to avoid interference from transmissions in channel 60.

A coalition of broadcasters, known as the Spectrum Clearing Alliance, developed a plan whereby the broadcasters would vacate both commercial and public safety spectrum on an expedited schedule.[75] The proposal by the Spectrum Clearing Alliance was for the commercial bands of the Upper 700 MHz spectrum to be auctioned to the wireless telecommunications companies; these companies would then negotiate with the current (broadcaster) occupants for a speedy vacating of the newly-licensed bands. This scenario is based on the assumption that the value of the spectrum to the wireless companies will be such that they will be motivated to pay the broadcasters to surrender the spectrum in a timely manner. The Spectrum Clearing Alliance also wanted to be able to relocate from the Upper 700 MHz band to the Lower 700 MHz band, if needed.

On March 19-20, 2002, the FCC issued separate auction notices setting the date of June 19, 2002 for both bands in the 700 MHz range. In late April and early May, bills were introduced in the House and Senate respectively[76] to postpone both auctions. On June 19, 2002, President Bush signed into law the Auction Reform Act of 2002[77] which delays auctions for all of the Upper 700 MHz band and most of the Lower 700 MHz band. Among provisions of the law is the requirement that the FCC file an annual status report on its actions in accordance with the Act.[78]

In the meantime, Chairman Powell announced a "Proposal for Voluntary Industry Action" that would expedite the transition to digital TV.[79] The proposal set goals for voluntary action to include DTV-tuners in new television sets. Later, citing provisions of the All Channel Receiver Act (1962) that gives the FCC "authority to require" that television sets receive all frequencies,[80] the FCC mandated a comparable schedule for the roll-out of DTV technology.[81] Legislation introduced in the 108th Congress (H.R. 426) would bar the FCC from taking this action without Congressional approval. DTV penetration of American households remains low, between 2% and 3%, as estimated by the Consumer Electronics Association.

Although the action by the FCC will facilitate the transition to digital technology, many industry observers doubt that this action will mitigate the "15% rule" that effectively allows broadcasters to retain spectrum after the 2006 date set by Congress. According to one attorney who represents cable television companies "it will take an act of Congress" to move forward.[82]

## *An Alternate Proposal*

The CTIA has circulated a concept paper[83] proposing that various federal law enforcement agencies relocate to the Upper 700 MHz band from other spectrum bands (that, consequently, would be freed for commercial wireless). The CTIA asserted that federal and state public agencies could benefit from a harmonized block of spectrum and that the Upper 700 MHz band could be used to support the advanced services, such as mobile data, that the National Coordinating Committee plans to implement as spectrum becomes available in the channels already assigned to public safety.

The CTIA concept paper envisioned that federal and state public safety agencies would benefit from shared systems that allow for the pooling of spectrum resources, increased efficiency in spectrum use, and accelerated deployment of new technologies. The paper also argued for the elimination of "antiquated" analog systems that are perceived as a barrier to implementing interoperable technology. It suggested that spectrum currently used for analog frequencies would become available for auction if public safety systems were fully converted to digital technologies. Funds from this auction, according to the paper, would pay for the costs of relocating federal agencies to a common platform in the Upper 700 MHz band. These recommendations have been revisited in CTIA proposals to mitigate interference, discussed in the next section.

In arguing for a "seamless, digital communications system founded on interoperability, mobility, security and multi-user connectivity" the CTIA's concept paper proposed that such a network be created in the Upper 700 MHZ band by the, then, White House Homeland Security Office. Homeland Security would coordinate the existing efforts of federal, state and local agencies, the NTIA, the FCC, and other organizations, such as PSWN.

## *Interoperability Trends*

The PSWN Program has identified recent trends in interoperability at the state level, where the issue is achieving greater recognition than in the past.[84] PSWN has observed that states are key linchpins in achieving interoperability. Among the trends summarized by PSWN are:

- States are organizing committees to provide leadership on interoperability issues.
- Existing statewide efforts to improve interoperability have been jeopardized by state budget shortfalls.
- The number of compatible statewide systems (APCO's Project 25) continues to increase.

- Where funding is available, states are beginning to purchase communications solutions that bolster interoperability.
- Planning continues for the implementation of shared, statewide public safety systems.

# Interference and Access: 800 MHz

Public safety currently uses 9.5 MHz of spectrum in the 800 MHz range at 806-821MHz and 851-869 MHz. At the behest of the National Public Safety Planning Advisory Committee (NPSPAC), frequencies at 821-824 MHz and 866-869 MHz, referred to as the "NPSPAC channels," are reserved for special public safety uses, such as interoperability. These frequencies are in 115 MHz of spectrum reallocated by the FCC in 1970 for land mobile use in the 806-947 MHz band.

The allocation of this spectrum interleaves public safety and private commercial communications using narrow slices of spectrum. This close proximity of public and commercial utilization is widely believed to be the primary cause of interference for communications by public safety and other entities using 800 MHz channels. Across the United States, there have been numerous reports of police or fire units that have lost contact with their base commands when a wireless connection was broken.[85] The problem has become sufficiently troublesome that APCO[86] has established a committee that operates nationwide to identify cases of interference.

## *Interference and Interoperability Issues Converge*

Although many wireless carriers have been involved in resolving problems of interference, a large number of the identified cases of interference have been linked to operations of Nextel Communications, Inc. To address the problem, Nextel prepared a White Paper[87] regarding use of the 800 MHz band and submitted it to the FCC in November 2001. The FCC subsequently assigned the paper a docket number. Comments on public safety communications uses in the 800 MHz band and related issues were sought by the FCC through September 23, 2002. Numerous solutions, some of which are summarized below, have been proposed. Amendments, replies and *Ex Parte* comments are still being submitted.[88] By late March 2003, approximately 600 documents had been filed with the FCC on issues raised by Nextel and others.

The detailed proposals for mitigating interference involve relocation within the 800 MHz band and to other frequency bands. Some of these proposals are highly technical, some are limited to discussions of policy. Although, to date, there appears to be no industry-wide consensus, there are some points where opinions converge, these include:

- There must be a nationwide program that identifies and eliminates causes of interference.
- Relocation is inevitable and this will require the retuning or replacement of existing equipment plus, in some cases, the modifications or expansion of network systems.
- Relocation will be expensive; estimates provided in comments range from $1.6 to $5 billion, nationwide.
- The issue of interference should be addressed within the context of larger issues relating to public safety and critical infrastructure such as interoperability.

Opinions diverge on such policy issues as how to pay for relocation, the permissible level of disruption to users — including industrial applications, equitable allocation of spectrum, and the amounts and frequency locations of spectrum that should be relocated.

### Requests for Congressional Action

Proposals that rely on relocating public safety users to channels at 700 MHz have emphasized the need to assure that this spectrum is made available on a timely basis and have asked for Congress to intervene. Some proposals have advocated allocating additional spectrum in the 700 MHz range and this also would require an act of Congress to modify existing law. Funding the cost of relocation is much discussed in the filed comments; Congressional action to create an appropriate funding mechanism is suggested by some. Some proposals would free up spectrum in the 800 MHz range that could be auctioned, and some have suggested that these funds be used to cover relocation costs. Since spectrum auction proceeds now go primarily to general revenue, new legislation would be needed that specifically addresses this matter.[89]

### Nextel's Proposal

In the letter to the FCC that accompanied the White Paper,[90] Nextel specifically attributed interference problems to earlier actions by the FCC "authorizing public safety communications providers and [commercial] licensees to operate essentially incompatible systems on mixed, interleaved and adjacent 800 MHz channels . . . Intermodulation is the dominant cause of interference, with wideband noise and receiver overload playing a secondary role." In the paper, Nextel presented a plan for spectrum realignment that would place public safety and commercial mobile radio services (CMRS) in separate blocks of contiguous spectrum. Nextel argued that the root cause of interference is the manner in which the spectrum has been allocated and that changing the allocation will eliminate the problem.

Among the benefits for public safety that are cited by Nextel in its paper is that the realigned blocks of spectrum will provide enough contiguous spectrum to support low-speed data, high-speed data, and video, as recommended by PSWN. Nextel's proposal received support from at least seven public safety agencies,[91] representatives of which wrote to the FCC (November 21, 2001) endorsing the proposal if it could be implemented at no cost to public safety agencies. Subsequently, most of these agencies joined with a number of industry associations and Nextel in designing an alternative plan, described in their filing as the "Consensus Plan."

The plan proposed that Nextel swap 16 MHz of spectrum it currently holds in the 700, 800, and 900 MHz bands in order to allow migration of current users from key parts of the 800 MHz band.[92] Public safety would be moved to spectrum in the 800 MHz range that is contiguous to channels 68-69,[93] gaining an additional 8 MHz of spectrum in the process. Nextel would occupy 6 MHz in the 800 MHz band currently used for public safety that is adjacent to a 10 MHz block that Nextel already holds. This realignment would create 16 MHz for digital Specialized Mobile Radio licensed to Nextel.

Under the Nextel plan, commercial licensees currently using the 800 MHz bands earmarked for public safety could continue operating on those frequencies with a secondary status, meaning they would have to stop broadcasting in times of high demand by public safety, or they could move to other frequencies. Spectrum in the 700 and 900 MHz ranges presently licensed by Nextel would be reassigned to displaced licensees for Specialized Mobile Radio services and for Business and Industrial/Land Transportation radio (B/ILT). As compensation for the surrendered bandwidth in the 700 and 900 MHz ranges, Nextel would get 10 MHz of spectrum in the 2 GHz Mobile Satellite Service (MSS) band.

To implement this plan, Nextel offered to contribute up to $500 million to help fund the costs of relocating public safety systems currently operating within the 800 MHz band. Nextel further proposed that the cellular operators and other license-holders that will be displaced should also "contribute substantially to the costs of relocating public safety licenses,"[94] since, Nextel asserted, they also will benefit from the proposed realignment.

## Business Users and Mobile Radio Operators

In order to achieve the realignment, Nextel has suggested that current occupants in the lower 800 MHz bandwidth for Specialized Mobile Radio (SMR) and for Business and Industrial/Land Transportation may have to relocate. Among private wireless users that would be affected by such a move are businesses that use these frequencies for internal communications, such as to monitor off-site activities, or for applications such as automatic reading of utility meters. Users include manufacturers, railroads, pipelines and utilities. Also impacted would be network operators such as Motient Corporation and Southern LINC[95] that provide wireless voice and data communications networks to businesses; Motient is also one of two networks used by BlackBerry [96] for its message service. Motient and Southern LINC are among the companies that have opposed Nextel's proposals.

## Proposal from the National Association of Manufacturers

The National Association of Manufacturers (NAM)[97], along with MFARC[98], submitted an alternative relocation plan.[99] This plan provided for the consolidation of spectrum into wider bands, removing the problem of interleaving. It would also juxtapose B/ILT bandwidth with public safety bandwidth, segregating SMR uses such as Nextel's to reduce interference further.

The NAM-MFARC proposal stated that retuning within the 800 MHz band is possible and should be undertaken as the solution to end interference. Public safety users would move to 10 MHz of spectrum partly adjacent to channels 68-69. This would provide public safety with the benefit of a contiguous bandwidth, facilitating the development of new technologies, and would slightly increase the amount of spectrum for public safety use, although not by as much as with the Nextel proposal.

The Specialized Mobile Radio and Business and Industrial/Land Transportation license holders in the affected 800 MHz range would retune to other bands in the same range but would not have to choose between secondary status and relocation to 700MHz or 900 MHz frequencies, as Nextel proposed in its plan. In its letter, NAM states that "the cost to larger manufacturers of relocating . . . would be in the tens of millions of dollars." Sharing spectrum on a secondary basis "would cause major disruption and dislocation to thousands of manufacturing operations." The B/ILT applications in the 800 MHz range support operations for "productivity and worker safety." In some localities, the systems "form the backbone of mutual aid agreements with nearby police, fire and emergency medical services."

MRFAC also joined with the American Association of Railroads, American Petroleum Institute, Forest Industries Telecommunications, Industrial Communications and Aeronautical Radio, Inc (ARINC), among others, to protest Nextel's proposal in a letter to Chairman Powell.[100] The letter repeated the concerns raised by NAM regarding the high cost and the disruptive impact on American industry that would result if the Nextel plan were implemented. These associations (except NAM and MFARC) later endorsed the "Consensus Plan." NAM and MFARC were also part of a similar alliance that, as the Private Wireless Coalition, lobbied to halt the auction of Upper 700 MHz spectrum in 2002.[101]

## The FCC Response

In its *Notice of Proposed Rulemaking*[102] — which appeared several months after the Nextel and NAM proposals were received, but before many other proposals since filed — the FCC responded by reiterating and amplifying the problems of interference broached in Nextel's letter and White Paper. It noted that both the NAM and Nextel proposals would require vacating five "NPSPAC channels" used for interoperability at 866-869 MHz and that 1,320 public safety and NPSPAC licensed stations would have to be relocated. The Nextel proposal would also require 2,100 B/ILT and 1,100 SMR licensees to relocate; the NAM proposal would require some, but "significantly fewer," licensees to relocate.

In the notice, the FCC concluded "tentatively . . . that increasing levels of harmful interference to public safety communications on the 800 MHz band must be remedied." It invited comment on how to restructure the band "resolving interference with minimum disruption to existing services." The FCC further noted that a restructuring might increase the amount of spectrum available for public safety and asked for comments that supply "quantitative information on public safety agencies' needs for additional spectrum." It referred to the PSWAC 1996 report that included an assessment of spectrum needs for public safety but concluded that this information should be updated.

After an analysis of the proposals submitted by Nextel and NAM, the FCC gave an example of an alternative restructuring plan that might be used. The FCC suggested that the problems of interference caused by interleaving could be eliminated by removing public safety communications from those bands. Seventy public safety channels would be placed in contiguous spectrum from 809.75-811.50 MHz. One hundred B/ILT channels would be relocated and 80 SMR channels would be moved. It sought comment on whether, if Public Safety, B/ILT, or SMR stations are relocated to new frequencies, there might be an opportunity to use spectrum more efficiently, for example by acquiring narrowband digital equipment to replace broadband.

Improving spectrum efficiency is one possible benefit of relocation within or from the 800 MHz range. The FCC also viewed relocation as an opportunity to provide additional channels for interoperability. In a discussion of relocation costs, the FCC reviewed several different approaches that have been used in previous instances and asked for comments on the matter. Notably, the question is posed as to whether — assuming some spectrum is recovered as a result of the relocation —the funds from auctioning recovered spectrum might be applied to the costs of relocation; alternatively, the FCC could require that winning bidders assume the costs of relocating public safety stations as a prerequisite for receiving the license.

### *Coalition for Constructive Public Safety Solutions*

A detailed proposal from an industry coalition offered a different approach, and guidelines for needed legislation. Building industry consensus, Southern LINC, Alltell Corporation, and FIRST Cellular joined Cingular Wireless, AT&T Wireless and Nokia, a major supplier of mobile phones and networks.[103] The keystone of the plan was to use all of the Upper 700 MHz spectrum (channels 60-69) for public safety. Some of this would be allocated specifically for homeland security, priority access for wireless communications in an emergency, and critical infrastructure. Frequencies used by public safety agencies in the 800 MHz range would be vacated, with current users moving to 700 MHz frequencies. The vacated spectrum would be auctioned for commercial use, with the proceeds used to help pay for the relocation of public safety agencies from the 800 MHz band.

The proposal further recommended that broadcasters currently occupying channels 60-69 be required to vacate this spectrum not later than December 31, 2006. The proposal noted that this provision would require Congress to respond with enabling legislation. Reportedly, Congress also would need to designate the Upper 700 MHz band for public safety, provide for the reallocation of the 800 MHz bandwidth vacated by public safety, and provide that the auction revenues generated under the plan be made available for relocation costs. The coalition was among those organizations petitioning for delay of the planned auction of Upper 700 MHz spectrum.[104]

## Consensus Plan

A proposal that has reportedly received broad-based (but not unanimous) support was submitted by a collective of public safety organizations,[105] a group of industry associations,[106] and Nextel. Initial comments by these "Joint Commenters" were sent to the FCC on August 7, 2002. The FCC responded first by issuing a Public Notice soliciting comment on the "Consensus Plan"[107] and extending the comment period to September 23; and then by allowing further comments on other plans or proposals.[108] The commenters filed a substantive "amendment" to their plan on December 24, 2002 that responded to many criticisms of the original "Consensus Plan."

The plan as amended represents a modified relocation proposal that places public safety uses in contiguous 800 MHz spectrum adjacent to the 700 MHz band. The plan specifically does not recommend using 700 MHz to resolve problems of interference, citing the need for Congressional action to free up the needed spectrum. In the proposal submitted in August, Nextel reaffirmed its willingness to spend up to $500 million to cover relocation costs for public safety entities, primarily for retuning existing equipment and replacing equipment that could not be retuned. In the amended plan, Nextel increased the amount of its offer to $850 million and included B/ILT licensees.[109] Estimates of probable costs for relocation prepared by Nextel concluded that it would cost $698 million to relocate public safety frequencies and $129.6 million to move B/ILT Consequently, Nextel offered to provide up to $700 million for public safety relocation costs and $150 million for commercial licensee expenditures. This funding would be provided on the condition that the FCC grant Nextel a 10 MHz nationwide CMRS license at 1910-1915/1990-1995 in return for a total of 10 MHz that Nextel would relinquish in the 700, 800 and 900 MHz bands. Previously, Nextel had requested compensating bandwidth in the 2 GHz Mobile Satellite Service (MSS) band. This change of request triggered a new round of *ex parte* filings in protest. The 1910-1915 MHz and 1930-1990 bands are presently used for unlicenced PCS use. Filings expressed concern and even outrage over the possibility of interference from Nextel transmissions in these frequencies.

Criticisms of the original "Consensus Plan," by PSWN and others, included the plan's failure to address immediate interference needs or to provide detailed relocation plans. The December 2002 amendments addressed these and other issues. Because of the extensive nature of these amendments, the FCC reopened the period for public comment, eventually accepting comments into May 2003.

## Other Proposals

The CTIA and the members of the Coalition for Public Safety Solutions have lead the protest against the Nextel and "Consensus Plan" proposals. As has the Coalition, the CTIA has advocated using 700 MHz frequencies for public safety. They have urged that all the Upper 700 MHz band be turned over for public safety and critical infrastructure uses. While not submitting a detailed proposal, CTIA has urged the FCC to respond with a "cohesive action plan" to mitigate interference. Such a plan would include moving public safety users and B/ILT from 800 MHz to the 700 MHz band — an interim step would require rebanding within 800 MHz to mitigate interference — and ways to improve public safety equipment and interference mitigation efforts. A two-phase transition —rebanding within the 800 MHZ frequencies to eliminate interleaving followed by migration to 700 MHZ — would, the CTIA has concluded, occur over a period of three to eight years, easing funding pressures. The CTIA has maintained that it is "irresponsible" of the FCC to address problems in the 800 MHz band without including uses at 700 MHz and the need for more spectrum for public safety. The CTIA has recommended that the 800 MHz frequencies used by public safety and B/ILT be auctioned, with the proceeds used to cover costs of relocation. Specifically, CTIA has stipulated that no commercial wireless carriers be "required" to cover relocation expenditures due to rebanding. Among other specific recommendations, CTIA joined Motorola and others in suggesting that public safety should acquire dual-band radios to improve efficiency.

Motorola, Inc. has filed multiple comments and proposals with the FCC for this docket, including several presentations explaining the causes of interference. Motorola is a major supplier of telecommunications equipment to the public safety sector and also to Nextel, which uses Motorola's iDEN technology for its commercial mobile wireless services. Motorola has suggested a rebanding approach that places public safety users at the lower end of the 800 MHz spectrum, adjacent to the Upper 700 MHz bands. Motorola has provided a plan that would give public safety up to 60 MHz of spectrum in the 700-800 MHz range, most of it contiguous. Its plan does not free up spectrum for auction. Motorola has argued that its plan maintains existing public safety investment in equipment using 800 MHz frequencies. Motorola has recognized that its approach will require a "high level of frequency coordination" and that many case-by-case decisions will be needed to mitigate interference. In its comments, it urged that problems with interference be further eased through the adoption of the "Best Practices

Guide," developed by APCO's Project 39, used during the Winter Olympic Games at Salt Lake City.

APCO submitted comments jointly with the National Association of Counties, the National League of Cities, and the National Association of Telecommunications Officers and Advisors.[110] Among other issues, this filing addresses the FCC's request for comments regarding the validity of PSWAC's estimates of spectrum needed for public safety. APCO et al. reported that the PSWAC findings regarding public safety are "largely accurate" but that demand for spectrum in the public safety sector may have been underestimated. APCO comments, therefore, stated that plans to reconfigure the 800 MHz must address both reduction in interference and additional spectrum for public safety use within the 800 MHz band. The comments cited a more recent analysis by APCO that concluded that an additional 32 MHz of spectrum, beyond the 95 MHz recommended by PSWAC, will be required. The comments also took the position that any plan should include " a mechanism to reimburse all of the implementation costs incurred by public safety licenses."

### *Cost of Relocation*

Some comments and proposals submitted to the FCC included estimates of the cost of relocation. The amounts of these estimates depended on differing assumptions for variables such as the extent of the rebanding and relocation and the cost of replacing or retuning existing equipment. As noted above, NAM estimated relocation costs for large manufacturers at "tens of millions" of dollars. In detailed analyses[111] presented in support of the "Consensus Plan," Nextel estimated costs of $698 million to relocate public safety frequencies and $129.6 million to move commercial and B/ILT uses. Nextel assumed that 10% of public safety radios would need replacement.

Motorola prepared cost estimates for the Nextel and NAM plans.[112] For the Nextel proposal, Motorola estimated relocation costs for public safety at $1.1 to $ 1.5 billion; the estimated cost for B/ILT and others was put at $1.7 to $2.4 billion. Total costs of relocation under Nextel's proposal would, according to Motorola's calculations, range from $2.8 to $3.9 billion. The estimates Motorola provided for the NAM proposal totaled $1.6 to $2.2 billion. The cost to public safety agencies would range from $1.1 to $1.5 billion; costs for B/ILT would be $500 to $700 million. To prepare these estimates, Motorola assumed that all equipment operating on 800 MHz frequencies would have to be retuned or replaced, and that 30-40% of radios would have to be replaced. The spread in the estimates was attributed to uncertainties such as the number of times a system might have to be moved in order to maintain full radio coverage during the rebanding. The lower estimates are based on changing frequencies only once. Another variable that could impact determining the cost of relocation depends on the number of radios actually in use by public safety agencies. Motorola used the FCC license database to estimate this number.

APCO has concluded that the FCC license database used by Motorola in preparing its cost estimates is not accurate enough for this purpose.[113] Further, APCO has concluded that the cost of implementing the necessary reprogramming of radios is unknown. APCO argued, therefore, that there should be no arbitrary limit on the amount of reimbursable costs although it concurred with the FCC that there should be guidelines for reimbursable costs. APCO also commented on the complexity of the task of distributing funds that may be set aside for public safety agency relocation costs. An administrative structure will be required. A key issue is matching reimbursable needs to available funds. APCO recommended that there be assurances that funds are available before public safety agencies incur relocation costs. There is also the related question of sufficient funding to cover all relocation costs. Would agencies be reimbursed on a "first come, first served" basis or would the administering agency prioritize funding, and, if so, using what criteria?

Other commenters citing cost concerns included the County of Maui, Hawaii, with a projection of $5 billion, nationwide.[114] Maui's estimate is based on its own costs for retuning a recently-acquired 800 MHz system and assumes that, among other costs, all radios will have to be retuned or replaced. The County of Maui filing urged that any relocation reimbursement plan should include the costs of planning for systems that would be abandoned as a result of rebanding.

## Critical Infrastructure Industries

By suggesting that B/ILT licensees be moved from the 800 MHz range to the 900 MHz range, the Nextel proposal also brought new attention to bear on another proposal before the FCC: a request to merge separate Business and Industrial/Land Transportation allocations into a single pool accessible to both services.[115] A related issue is the possible designation of a portion of the 900 MHz band for use by Critical Infrastructure Industries (CII).[116] Critical infrastructure has been defined as "electric, gas and water utilities, petroleum and natural gas pipelines and railroads." The FCC has asked for comment on these two matters in the same notice and with the same time frame as its request for input regarding 800 MHz spectrum use.

The FCC had previously resisted a request to designate spectrum specifically for critical infrastructure, as this would not be efficient use of spectrum.[117] Key issues surrounding the use of spectrum by CII have been recently addressed by the NTIA[118] and also studied by the FCC as required by Congress.[119]

### *Critical Infrastructure Industries and Intelligent Transportation Systems*

The FCC has proposed to provide spectrum at 5.9 GHz to support Intelligent Transportation Systems (ITS)[120] using public safety Dedicated Short Range Communications (DSRC) services. In its *Notice of Proposed Rule Making and Order,[121]* the FCC proposed to move ahead with standards for ITS at 5.9 GHz and requested comments on technical and administrative issues. In the *Notice,* the FCC reaffirmed earlier decisions to treat ITS as a public safety use of spectrum, not as a commercial use. Further, it linked ITS to critical infrastructure industries and sought comment regarding the definition of public safety services contained in the Communications Act of 1934.[122] The definition sets a narrow standard for public safety services that generally eliminate CII uses; however, the FCC has argued that other provisions of the Act can be interpreted to cover CII.

The Communications Act defines public safety services as "services, including private internal radio services, used by state and local governments and non-government entities, and including emergency road services provided by not-for-profit organizations that are (i) used to protect the safety of life, health, or property; and (ii) are not made commercially available to the public."[123] Users of these services are exempt from the FCC's auction authority; included in this group are utilities, railroads, metropolitan transit systems, pipelines and private ambulance services.

## Multiple Address Systems at 900 MHz

Multiple Address Systems (MAS) is a radio communication service located in the 900 MHz band. The FCC has designated 20 channels in the 932-941 MHz band exclusively for the use of public safety and federal government agencies as well as some private internal uses, licensed on a site-by-site basis. Also, bands at 928/952/956 MHz are designated for sharing between private and public users.[124] Present proposals regarding reallocation in the 800 MHz and 900 MHz bands, summarized above, do not discuss relocating any MAS channels.

## Full Broadband Capabilities: 4.9 GHz

In response to pressure from public safety organizations and other concerned parties, the FCC has designated 50 MHz of spectrum at 4.9 GHz[125] for fully-interoperable broadband applications for public safety, including short-range broadband Wireless Local Networks (WLANs). Many mission-critical applications are envisioned. PAN/VAN systems can provide customized, hands-free links between a portable, wireless base station and devices that might be integrated into helmets or suits, such as headsets, portable computers, video cameras, thermal imagers, sensors and 3D locators. WLAN on-scene/incident command networks can carry real-time multimedia wireless communications. Wireless fixed "hot spot" locations can support high speed transfers of data, image and video files.

In the *Second Report and Order*[126] announcing its decision to allocate spectrum at 4.9 MHz to public safety instead of auctioning it for commercial use, the FCC explored pertinent issues and requested comments on various policy and technical decisions. Policy issues identified by the FCC included: eligibility for using the spectrum; allowing some access to commercial wireless service providers; steps to promote spectral efficiency; and international harmonization.

In its subsequent *Third Report and Order*,[127] the FCC ruled that primary access would be restricted to the definition of public safety services as defined by the amended Communications Act of 1934.[128] This definition will preclude licensing frequencies to critical infrastructure industries, among others. The *Order*, however, has given considerable leeway to public safety agencies that want to lease or share bandwidth in the 4.9 MHz band. Furthermore, the FCC encouraged "public safety licensees to work with non-traditional public safety users, such as utilities, to implement new communications systems in support of public safety operations."[129]

## Future Technologies: Ultra-wide Band

In February 2003, the FCC reaffirmed rules and procedures, promulgated the previous year, that permit limited deployment of ultra-wideband (UWB) wireless technologies for public safety and some other uses in higher spectrum frequencies.[130] UWB sends ultra low power pulses over a broad range of the spectrum whereas traditional wireless technology operates on a specific frequency. The comparatively new and untested nature of the technology has raised concerns about interference with other wireless transmissions. Initially, certain types of products using UWB will be allowed to operate at frequencies primarily in the 3.1 GHz to10.6 GHz range. The limited applications are based on standards developed by the NTIA with the objective of protecting various government operations from interference; the FCC will review these standards and possibly explore more flexible requirements that will permit wider usage of UWB.[131]

Federal concerns about interference from UWB have centered on satellite systems, notably the Global Positioning System (GPS), and aviation safety for air navigation. The commercial wireless industry has also expressed concern about interference, both with wireless calls and with GPS-assisted technology being implemented for wireless enhanced 911 (E911).[132] The Association of Public-Safety Communications Officials (APCO) wrote the FCC to express concern over UWB.[133] Possible interference in bands below 6 GHZ present an "unacceptable risk" to public safety operations, the letter reads. "Within buildings, low-power public safety radios (all of which operate below 1 GHz) may be susceptible to signal degradation caused by increased noise levels produced by UWB devices." Additional interference to communications in the 800 MHz band was also mentioned as a concern. The letter reiterated wireless carriers concerns regarding the possible impact on the proper functioning of some wireless E911 systems.

The Department of Transportation reportedly requested that, to avoid interference, the lower limit for UWB be set at 6.1 GHz, while the Department of Defense (DOD) had suggested 4.1 GHz as the threshold.[134] While the Department of Transportation and the National Aeronautical and Space Administration (NASA) reportedly continue to oppose the FCC's decision at a time when air safety has become a national priority,[135] the DOD concluded that the "FCC's technical restrictions on UWB devices would be sufficient to protect military systems."[136]

Initial applications of UWB for public safety include ground penetration and through-wall imaging systems; commercial use of these technologies, such as for mining and construction will also be permitted. Other potential commercial applications include consumer appliances that use short-distance wireless communications such as presently used for cordless phones.

The three types of UWB devices that will be permitted under the current FCC rules are: 1) imaging systems using Ground Penetrating Radars (GPRs), wall, through-wall, medical imaging, and surveillance devises, 2) vehicular radar systems, and 3) communication and measurement systems.[137] For imaging systems — GPRs can detect or obtain images of buried objects by directing energy into the ground. Wall imaging systems similarly locate objects within a "wall," which could be a building, bridge or mine, for example. Permitted users for these two imaging applications are law enforcement, fire and rescue organizations, scientific research organizations, commercial mining companies, and construction companies. Through-wall imaging systems can detect location or movement on the opposite side of a structure. Use is restricted to law enforcement and fire and rescue. UWB medical imaging systems can be used under the supervision of a licensed health care practitioner. The FCC has classified UWB surveillance systems as imaging technology for the purposes of regulation. These systems depend on the transmission of radio frequencies to detect movement within a defined perimeter; they may be used by public utilities and other industries as well as by law enforcement and fire and rescue.

The FCC has provided for the operation of vehicular radar systems on ground transportation vehicles using directional antennae with controlled emissions. This ruling enables the automobile industry to continue with the development of vehicular radio systems in the 24GHz band. Also known as short-range radar (SRR), the technology can help drivers avoid collisions and prevent certain accidents such as backing over a child while exiting a garage; the technology can also be used to improve airbag activation and suspension systems.[138]

UWB communications and measurement systems permitted by the FCC under the ruling include high-speed home and business networks and industry applications such as storage tank measurement. In general this application is limited by the FCC to indoors operations and peer-to-peer communications on handheld devices.

The FCC is continuing its testing of UWB devices. Reportedly, it has found ambient noise levels in affected spectrum that significantly exceed the interference threshold established for UWB emissions.[139] Signaling its support of the nascent technology, the FCC recently hosted technology demonstrations of UWB devices.[140]

## REVIEW OF RECENT ACTIVITY IN CONGRESS

Authorization of appropriations for pilot programs for interoperable wireless communications at the state level was provided in a bill introduced in the 107th Congress by Senator Ron Wyden (S. 2037). An initial hearing,[141] on the role of technology in meeting the crisis of September 11, identified interoperability, spectrum capacity and wireless interference as key problems.

As originally introduced by Senator Wyden, the bill would have created a pool of technology experts and industry leaders (National Emergency Technology Guard or NET Guard) who would be prepared to provide resources in a national emergency, working with FEMA, funded at $5 million. The bill also would have funded seven state pilots to develop interoperable systems, at $5 million each, chosen in consultation with the Public Safety Wireless Network, under the auspices of the United States Fire Administration. In addition, the National Institute of Standards and Technology (NIST) would have received $35,000,000 to support programs for innovative technologies relating to security and emergency response. The bill also called for a report to the Congress regarding policy options and with recommendations to ensure that emergency officials and first responders have access to effective and reliable communications capabilities. The bill, significantly amended, was approved by the Senate on July 19, 2002 and reported to the House. Subsequently, the Homeland Security Act included the opportunity to create NET Guard within DHS, under the supervision of the Under Secretary for Information Analysis and Infrastructure Protection.[142] The under secretary may establish a "national technology guard . . . comprised of local teams of volunteers with expertise in relevant areas of science and technology." Their purpose would be to "assist in response and recovery from attacks on information systems and communications networks." Funding programs that would support interoperability were eliminated.

Concerns about spectrum management, especially as regards spectrum used for public safety, prompted the introduction of H. R. 4560, the Auction Reform Act of 2002, on April 24, 2002. The primary objective of the bill was to postpone auctions for the Upper and Lower 700 MHz bands originally scheduled by the FCC for June 19, 2002. (See discussion of issues under Interoperability: Upper 700 MHz Band.) Shepherded through the House by Members Dingell and Tauzin, the bill was introduced in the Senate in May and placed on the calendar on May 17, 2002. On May 2, 2002, Senator John Ensign had introduced a related bill, S. 2454. The Senate acted quickly and compromise legislation became P.L.107-195 on June 19, 2002.

In the 108th Congress, Representative Tauzin and Senator McCain have introduced complementary bills (H.R. 1320 and S. 865) to create a spectrum relocation fund, discussed above. The bill was amended during committee markup to include language specifying that spectrum being relocated from federal users could be allocated to public safety. After passage by the House, the bill was passed in mark up by the Senate Committee on Commerce, Science and Transportation. The addition of a controversial amendment that would benefit Northpoint Communications reportedly could harm the bill's chances for passage by the Senate.[143] Both Senator McCain and Representative Tauzin have expressed dismay over the inclusion of the amendment. [144]

To provide spectrum for interoperability at frequencies for which standards have been developed, legislation has been introduced by Congressman Jane Harman to mandate the timely clearing of Upper 700 MHz spectrum in the channels designated for public safety. This bill was originally introduced in the 107th Congress and has been reintroduced in the 108th Congress as H.R. 1425. A bill that would prevent the FCC from requiring new televisions to accommodate digital signals — part of the FCC's efforts to accelerate the transition to digital television and the clearing of 700 MHz bands — is the intent of H.R. 426 (Sensenbrenner).

Provisions that could significantly impact emergency communications, but not decisions about spectrum, are included in S. 930, H.R. 1449, and H.R. 105, among others.

## ENDNOTES

[1]   Federal Communications Commission (FCC), Notice of Proposed Rulemaking and Order, released November 15, 2002 (WT Docket No. 01-90).

[2]   CRS reports covering policy and funding issues related to first responders include CRS Report RS21400, *FY2003 Appropriations for First Responder Preparedness: Fact Sheet* and CRS Report RL31475, *First Responder Initiative: Policy Issues and Options*.

[3]   Better Coordination and Enhanced Accountability Needed to Improve Spectrum Management, GAO-02-906, September 30, 2002.

[4]   Comprehensive Review of U.S. Spectrum Management with Broad Stakeholder Involvement Is Needed, GAO-03-277, January 31, 2003.

[5]   See CRS Report RS21469, The National Telecommunications and Information Administration (NTIA): Budget, Programs, and Issues.

[6]   "Balanced Budget Act of 1997," P.L.107-33, Title III.

[7]   "Top Tauzin Aide Outlines Panel's Agenda for Next Congress," National Journal's Congress Daily, November 15, 2002

[8]  This and other special funds are discussed in CRS Report RS21508, Spectrum Management: Special Funds.

[9]  Geographic Information Systems, administered in part by FEMA.

[10]  See CRS Report RL31873, Homeland Security: Banking and Financial Infrastructure Continuity.

[11]  "Fatal Confusion: A Troubled Emergency Response" New York Times, July 7, 2002.

[12]  Standard abbreviations for measuring frequencies include: kHz — kilohertz or thousands of hertz; MHz — megahertz, or millions of hertz; and GHz — gigahertz, or billions of hertz.

[13]  Very High Frequency (VHF) and Ultra High Frequency (UHF) are transmitted in three bands in the United States — low VHF, high VHF and UHF.

[14]  Frequency ranges 25-50 MHz; 150-174 MHz; 220-222 MHz (shared with federal agencies); 421-430 (three urban areas); 450-470 MHz; and 470-512 MHz (11 urban areas).

[15]  Member agencies include the Departments of Homeland Security, Treasury, Defense, Justice, Commerce, State, Interior, Agriculture, Health and Human Services, Homeland Security, Energy, Veterans Affairs and Transportation as well as the CIA, Federal Emergency Management Agency, The Joint Staff, General Services Administration, National Aeronautics and Space Administration, Nuclear Regulatory Commission, National Security Agency, U.S. Postal Service, Federal Reserve Board, the FCC, and the NTIA. See [http://www.ncs.gov].

[16]  CS Press Release, "NCS Begins Deployment of Nationwide Wireless Priority Service," January 21, 2003. [http://www.ncs.gov].

[17]  Communications Daily, "SBC Executive Urges Industry to Coordinate Standards Initiatives," February 5, 2003.

[18]  "Final Report of the Public Safety Wireless Advisory Committee," September 11, 1996 [http://ntiacsd.ntia.doc.gov/ pubsafe/final.htm].

[19]  "Balanced Budget Act of 1997," P.L.105-33, Title III.

[20]  See [http://www.pswn.gov/about.htm].

[21]  The PSWN Program is administered jointly by the Departments of Justice and the Treasury. The Program is scheduled to end in 2010 [http://www.pswn.gov].

[22]  "Petition for Rule Making to Promote the Allocations of Spectrum for Public Safety Agencies . . ." PSWN, September 14, 2001 [http://www.fcc.gov/e-file/ecfs.html].

[23]  See, for example, "4.9 GHz: A Public Safety Spectrum Opportunity," ex parte filing July 31, 2001 regarding FCC WT Docket 00-32, by John

Lyons, Motorola Government Relations, Washington, DC [http://www.fcc.gov/e-file/ecfs.html].

24  "Land Mobile Replacement Cost Study," June 1998, [http://www.pswn.gov].

25  "E-government solutions are prominently represented in efforts to improve the management and efficiency of government information technology resources." CRS Report RL31057, A Primer in E-Government.

26  "FEMA Takes Lead for Broader Public Safety Wireless Program," Communications Daily, June 10, 2002.

27  "Homeland Security Starting Over with SAFECOM," Government Computer News, June 9, 2003.

28  "SafeCom Gets New Home," Federal Computer Week, April 8, 2003.

29  See [http://wireless.fcc.gov/publicsafety/700MHz/regional.html].

30  Kathleen Wallman, Chair of the Public Safety National Coordination Committee (NCC), conversation June 26, 2002

31  See [http://www.fcc.gov/hspc].

32  See [http://www.fcc.gov/hspc/HSPC_functions.pps].

33  Council Charter, see [http://www.nric.org]

34  Homeland Security Public Safety (Focus Group 1C) Final Report, Issue 1, March 2003 [http://www.nric.org/].

35  See [http://www.mediasecurity.org].

36  FCC News, "Homeland Security: Industry Leaders Consider Emergency Communications and Public Warning System Recommendations," May 28, 2003 [http://www.fcc.gov].

37  Spectrum Policy Task Force Report, ET Docket 02-135, November 2002. See [http://www.fcc.gov/sptf].

38  Comments can be found by going to the FCC Electronic Comment Filing System (ECFS) on the FCC web site [http://www.fcc.gov]. In ECFS, click "Search for Filed Comments," insert "02-135" in the box marked "Proceeding," and then search the file.

37  Spectrum Policy Task Force Report, ET Docket 02-135, November 2002. See [http://www.fcc.gov/sptf].

38  Comments can be found by going to the FCC Electronic Comment Filing System (ECFS) on the FCC web site [http://www.fcc.gov]. In ECFS, click "Search for Filed Comments," insert "02-135" in the box marked "Proceeding," and then search the file.

37  Spectrum Policy Task Force Report, ET Docket 02-135, November 2002. See [http://www.fcc.gov/sptf].

[38] Comments can be found by going to the FCC Electronic Comment Filing System (ECFS) on the FCC web site [http://www.fcc.gov]. In ECFS, click "Search for Filed Comments," insert "02-135" in the box marked "Proceeding," and then search the file.

[39] Filed, January 27, 2003, ET Docket 02-135.

[40] IRAC, with representation from 20 major federal agencies, develops policies for federal spectrum use, and represents the United States at International Telecommunications Union conferences. http://www.ntia. dov.gov/osmhome/irac.htm/.

[41] Summary of the symposiumat [http://ntiacsd.ntia.doc.gov/pubsafe/TIS_FinalReport.pdf].

[42] Discussed in CRS Report RS 21469, The National Telecommunications and Information Administration (NTIA): Budget, Programs, and Issues.

[43] See [http://www.disa.mil/ops/os/os.html].

[44] For further information, see CRS Report RL313670, Transfer of FEMA to the Department of Homeland Security: Issues for Congressional Oversight.

[45] See also CRS Report RS21440, Emergency Communications: The Emergency Alert Service (EAS) and All-Hazard Warnings.

[46] See "Developing a Unified All-Hazard Public Warning System," Partnership for Public Warning, McLean, VA, PPW Report 2002-02, November 25, 2002. [http://www.partnershipforpublicwarning.org].

[47] Section 503 of P.L. 107-296.

[48] P.L. 105-119.

[49] P.L. 100-690, see [http://www.ojp.usdoj.gov/BJA/grant/byrne.html]

[50] See [http://www.ojp.usdoj.gov/BJA/grant/llebg_app.html].

[51] Title II, sections 231-237 of P.L. 107-296.

[52] AGILE stands for Advanced Generation of Interoperability for Law Enforcement. See [http://www.agileprograms.org].

[53] Member associations are: APCO-International, International Association of Chiefs of Police, International Association of Fire Chiefs, International City/County Management Association, Major Cities Chiefs Association, National Association of Counties, National Association of State Chief Information Officers, National Association of State Telecommunications Directors, National Conference of State Legislatures, National Criminal Justice Association, National Emergency Management Association, National Governors Association, National League of Cities, National Public Safety Telecommunications Council, National Sheriffs' Association, The Council of State

Governments, and The United States Conference of Mayors. See [http://www.agileprogram.org/ntfi/justnet.html].

[54] Sec. 103 (d) (2).

[55] Sec. 232 (6) (E).

[56] Sec. 201 (e) (19) (g) (2).

[57] Sec. 201 (e) (7).

[58] Sec. 502 (7).

[59] Federal Response Plan, 9230.1 PL, [http://www.fema.org/rrr/frp/].

[60] A Republican Approach to the Department of Homeland Security; recommendations for the first 100 days, Republican Main Street Partnership, released December 10, 2002. Available at [http://www. republicanmainstreet.org/rmsp/homeland.cfm].

[61] See [http://www.apcointl.org].

[62] See [http://npstc.du.edu].

[63] FCC, "Alternative Frequencies for Use by Public Safety Systems," 2002, [http://www.fcc.gov/hspc/].

[64] Floyd D. Spence National Defense Authorization Act for Fiscal Year 2001, P.L. 106-398.

[65] NTIA, "Alternative Frequencies for Use by Public Safety Systems," December 2001, [http://www.ntia.doc.gov].

[66] FCC, "Alternative Frequencies for Use by Public Safety Systems," 2002, [http://www.fcc.gov/hspc/].

[67] BNA, Inc. Daily Report for Executives, February 11, 2002, "DOD Agrees to Share Spectrum . . ." [http://ippubs.bna.com].

[68] Comments can be found by going to the FCC Electronic Comment Filing System (ECFS) on the FCC web site [http://www.fcc.gov]. In ECFS, click "Search for Filed Comments," insert "99-16" in the box marked "Proceeding," and then search the file.

[69] "Balanced Budget Act of 1997," P.L.105-33, Title III.

[70] 746-764 MHz.

[71] 776-794 MHz.

[72] See also CRS Report RL31260, Digital Television: An Overview.

[73] Opening remarks by Tom Sugrue, Chief, Wireless Telecommunications Bureau, FCC, at a General Membership Meeting of the FCC's Public Safety National Coordination Committee, Brooklyn, New York, November 15, 2001.

[74] Voluntary clearing of channels in advance of the 2006 "deadline" has been the primary focus of recent efforts by the FCC. In its Upper 700 MHz Third Report and Order (January 23, 2001), the FCC completed the adoption of policies to facilitate voluntary clearing of the 60-69

channels. Notably it allowed for three-way agreements (bi-lateral agreements had already been approved) that would allow incumbent broadcasters in the Upper 700 MHz range to relocate to channels below 59 in cases where these channels had already been vacated. In an "Order on Reconsideration" (September 17, 2001) the FCC reaffirmed the Third Report and Order and added new incentives to encourage agreements for incumbent broadcasters to vacate the affected spectrum. (WT Docket No. 99-168).

75 A broad outline of the band-vacating plan that would be provided by the Spectrum Clearing Alliance was submitted to the FCC on March 16, 2001. "The Spectrum Clearing Alliance Petition for Clarification and Recommendation," WT-Docket No. 99-168.

76 H.R. 4560 and S. 2454

77 P.L. 107-195

78 The first *Report to Congress* was released June 19, 2003 (FCC 03-138). [http://hraunfoss.fcc.gov/edocs_public/attachmatch/FCC-03-138A2.pdf].

79 Letter from FCC Chairman Michael Powell to Members of Congress, April 4, 2002, [http://www.fcc.gov].

80 FCC News release, "FCC Introduces Phase-In Plan for DTV Tuners," August 8, 2002.

81 Sets 36" and above - 50% of units to have DTV tuners by July 1, 2004; 100% by July 1, 2005. Sets 25"-35" - 50% of units to have DTV tuners by July 1,2005; 100% by July 1, 2006. Sets 13"-24" - 100% of units to have DTV tuners by July 1, 2007. TV interface devices - 100% of units to have DTV tuners by July 1, 2007.

82 Public Broadcasting Report, "Legal Experts Predict Congress Will Have to Step in on DTV," December 13, 2002.

83 "Homeland Emergency Response Operational Enhancement Systems (HEROES) Network," November 8, 2001, White Paper provided to CRS by the CTIA (202-785-0081).

84 PSWN Program Update, Fall 2002 [http://www.pswn.gov/].

85 The FCC states that the interference is "well documented." Notice of Proposed Rulemaking, released March 15, 2002, WT Docket No 02-55, (FCC Rcd 02-81).

86 Project 39 Technical Committee at [http://www.apcointl.org/frequency/project_39].

87 "Promoting Public Safety Communications: Realigning the 800 MHz Land Mobile Radio Band to Rectify Commercial Public Radio - Public Safety Interference and Allocate Additional Spectrum to Meet Critical

Public Safety Needs." Available at [http://www.fcc.gov/e-file/ecfs.html] under Nextel, docket numbers 00-258, 95-18, 99-81 or 99-87, dated November 21, 2001.

[88] Comments can be found by going to the FCC Electronic Comment Filing System (ECFS) on the FCC web site [http://www.fcc.gov]. In ECFS, click "Search for Filed Comments," insert "02-55" in the box marked "Proceeding," and then search the file.

[89] Similar funding measures are under consideration for federal agencies that must relocate. The Spectrum Relocation Fund is briefly discussed in the introductory section of this report under Issues for the 108th Congress.

[90] From Robert S. Foosaner, Senior Vice President and Chief Regulatory Officer, Nextel Communications, Inc., to Mr. Thomas Sugrue, Chief, Wireless Telecommunications Bureau, November 21, 2001.

[91] Association of Public-Safety Communications Officials (APCO) International; International Association of Fire Chiefs; International Association of Chiefs of Police; Major Cities Chiefs Associations; National Sheriffs' Association; Major County Sheriffs' Association; National Public Safety Telecommunications Council.

[92] The bandwidths that would be realigned in the Nextel proposal are 806-824 MHz and 851-869 MHz, a total of 36 MHz.

[93] Channels 68-69 are at 794-806 MHz.

[94] Nextel letter to FCC, op. cit.

[95] Southern Telecommunications Services, a division of Southern Company.

[96] Manufactured by Research in Motion.

[97] The National Association of Manufacturers represents 14,000 members, including 10,000 small and mid-sized companies and 350 member associations serving manufacturers and employees in every industrial sector and all 50 states.

[98] MFARC is one of the FCC's certified frequency coordinators for private land mobile bands from 150MHz to 900 MHz. Now an independent entity, MFARC was originally the frequency coordinating arm for NAM.

[99] Letter from Jerry J. Jasinowski, President, NAM to Michael Powell, Chairman, FCC, December 21, 2001.

[100] Letter of December 20, 2001 referred to as the "ARINC Letter."

[101] Letter to FCC, April 16, 2002; filed as comments regarding WT Docket 02-55.

[102] Notice of Proposed Rulemaking, released March 15, 2002, WT Docket No 02-55, (FCC Rcd 02-81).

[103] Several similar proposals were filed by the members of the "Coalition," jointly and separately, but not as the "Coalition." This title was used in their joint petition to Congress.

[104] Communications Daily, page 7, April 29, 2002.

[105] APCO-International; International Association of Chiefs of Police; International Association of Fire Chiefs, Inc.; International Municipal Signal Association; Major Cities Chiefs Association; Major County Sheriffs' Association; National Sheriffs' Association.

[106] ARINC; American Mobile Telecommunications Association; American Petroleum Institute; Association of American Railroads; Forest Industries Telecommunications; Industrial Telecommunications Association; National Stone, Sand and Gravel Association; Personal Communications Industry Association; Taxicab, Limousine and Paratransit Association.

[107] FCC, Public Notice, released September 6, 2002, DA 02-2202.

[108] FCC, Public Notice, released September 17, 2002, DA 02-2306.

[109] Supplemental Comments of the Consensus Parties, December 24, 2002, Appendix A, WT Docket 02-55.

[110] Filed May 6, 2002, WT Docket 02-55.

[111] "Consensus Plan" filing, December 24, 2002, Appendix A, WT Docket 02-55.

[112] Filed May 6, 2002, WT Docket 02-55.

[113] ibid.

[114] Filed May 6, 2002, WT Docket 02-55.

[115] "Petition for Rulemaking of the Personal Communications Industry Association," ("PCIA Petition"), filed November 14, 2001. The FCC created "pool categories" for B/ILT and SMR licenses in the 800MHz and 900 MHz ranges. "Intercategory sharing" was permitted in the 800MHz range — but was discontinued — and is still permitted in the 900 MHz range. A licensee unable to find a needed frequency in its designated category, or pool, can apply to the FCC for a frequency in another pool. The PCIA Petition requests that Business and Industrial/Light Transportation be placed in a single pool to create contiguous spectrum and to eliminate the costly and time-consuming waiver request process.

[116] On August 14, 1998, the American Petroleum Institute, the American Association of Railroads and the Telecommunications Council (now known as the United Telecom Council) filed a Petition for Rulemaking

(RM-9405) asking for such a set aside; this is known as the "UTC Proposal."

[117] Report and Order and Further Notice of Proposed Rulemaking, 15 FCC Rcd 22709.

[118] Department of Commerce, National Telecommunications and Information Administration, Current and Future Spectrum Use by the Energy, Water and Railroad Industries, January 2002.

[119] "Department of Commerce, Justice, and State, the Judiciary, and Related Agencies Appropriations Act, 2001," P.L. 106-553, Title II.

[120] ITS is discussed in CRS Report RL31283, "Intelligent Transportation Systems for Highway and Transit: Status, Federal Role, and Options for Reauthorization.

[121] FCC 02-302; WT Docket No. 01-90; released November 15, 2002.

[122] 47 U.S.C. § 337 (f)(1).

[123] In 1997 amendments to the Communications Act of 1934 , Congress defined public safety services as "services — (A) the sole or principal purpose of which is to protect the safety of life, health or property; (B) that are provided (i) by State or local government entities; or (ii) by nongovernmental organizations that are authorized by a governmental entity whose primary mission is the provision of such services ; and (C) that are not made commercially available to the public by the provider."

[124] Memorandum Opinion and Order, Released May 29, 2001, WT Docket No. 97-81.

[125] 4940 MHz-4990 MHz; fixed and mobile (excluding aeronautical mobile).

[126] Second Report and Order and Notice of Proposed Rulemaking, Released February 27, 2002, WT Docket No. 00-32 (FCC Rcd 02-47).

[127] Memorandum Opinion and Order and Third Report and Order, Released May 2, 2003, WT Docket No. 00-32 [http://www.fcc.gov].

[128] 47 U.S.C. § 337 (f)(1).

[129] "FCC Acts to Promote Homeland Security and the Development of Wireless Broadband Services in Support of Public Safety," FCC News, April 23, 2003 [http://www.fcc.gov].

[130] FCC, Memorandum Opinion and Order and Further Notice of Proposed Rule Making, February 12, 2003 reaffirmed its First Report and Order, February 14, 2002; clarified with Order, July 12, 2002 (ET Docket 98-153).

[131] FCC press release February 12, 2002, [http://www.fcc.gov].

[132] Wireless carriers and public safety answering points (PSAPs) are installing new technology to provide automatic number identification

and automatic location identification for wireless calls, similar to that already available for landline calls. See also, CRS Report RS21028, Emergency Communications: Wireless Enhanced 911 Issues Update.

[133] Letter dated January 16, 2002, as reported in FCC Report, January 25, 2002, "FCC News In Brief."

[134] Mobile Communications Report, Feb 18, 2002 "Commission Approves UWB Order, Agrees to Revisit Limits"

[135] RCR Wireless News, February 18, 2002, "Government, Carriers Decry UWB Order"

[136] Steven Price, Deputy Assistant Director for Spectrum and Communications, Department of Defense, quoted in Satellite Week, February 18, 2002, "Commission Approves UWB Order, Agrees to Revisit Limits."

[137] FCC press release, op. cit.

[138] See, for example, "Multifunction Automotive Radar Network (RadarNet)" at [http://radarnet.org/publications/].

[139] Communications Daily, January 16, 2003.

[140] FCC, Press Release, "FCC to Host Technology Demonstrations of New Ultra-Wideband Devices with Applications for Public Safety, Business, and Consumers," February 11, 2003.

[141] Senate Committee on Commerce, Science, and Transportation, Subcommittee on Science, Technology & Space, "Hearing on the Response of the Technology Sector in Times of Crisis," December 5, 2001.

[142] P.L. 107-296, Sec. 224.

[143] National Journal's Technology Daily, PM Edition, "Senate Commerce Committee Backs Spectrum Trust Fund," June 26, 2003.

[144] Communications Daily, "Northpoint Amendment Could Kill Spectrum Trust Fund Bill," June 27, 2003.

*Chapter 2*

# THE EMERGENCY ALERT SYSTEM (EAS) AND ALL-HAZARD WARNINGS

The two mainstays of the U.S. capacity to issue warnings are the Emergency Alert System (EAS), which relies primarily on broadcasting media, and the NOAA Weather Radio All-Hazards Network. The National Weather Service (NWS) of the National Oceanic and Atmospheric Administration (NOAA)[1] sends alerts through NOAA Weather Radio (NWR), now expanded to include warnings for all hazards. Several initiatives are underway within the federal government to improve, expand, and integrate existing warning systems. The most important of these — in terms of using, testing and developing leading-edge technology — is the Integrated Public Alert and Warning System (IPAWS), a public-private partnership in which the Department of Homeland Security (DHS) has a leadership role. Many communities, meanwhile, are installing local alert systems that send voice, text messages, and e-mail. Amber Alert[2] systems exist in most states to aid primarily in the recovery of abducted children.[3] Amber Alerts are currently supported by a number of different technologies, including a quasi-national network based on the Internet. Amber Alert messages also can be sent through the Emergency Alert System and the NOAA Weather Radio All-Hazards Network. Many agree that the long-term goal for emergency alerts is to converge federal warning systems into an integrated network that can interface with localized warning systems and also call centers, such as those used for 911 and 211 calls.[4]

*The 9/11 Commission Report* discusses the effectiveness of emergency alerts at the World Trade Center on September 11, 2001, with a focus on communications systems.[5] Recent, major studies of warning systems have concluded that the United States needs a more robust emergency alert system. Recommendations for improvement include using all available means of communication, providing a standardized alert protocol, and developing infrastructure for notification to geographically-specific locations and virtual communities.[6] A virtual community in the context of emergency communications refers to the technical ability to give immediate, simultaneous alerts to the appropriate community of responders and affected residents. Before its towers collapsed, the World Trade Center might have benefitted if virtual community or geo-targeted alert technology had been in place and activated.

## EAS ADMINISTRATION

EAS currently sends emergency messages with the cooperation of broadcast radio and television and most cable television stations. It was created as CONELRAD (Control of Electromagnetic Radiation) in 1951, as part of America's response to the threat of nuclear attack. In 1963, the system was opened to state and local participation. Through most of its existence, the alert system was known as the Emergency Broadcast System. The name was changed in the 1990's when the technology was upgraded and automated.

Congress has placed responsibility for civil defense measures that include the present-day EAS with the Director of the Federal Emergency Management Agency (FEMA)[7] now part of the Department of Homeland Security (DHS). The Federal Communications Commission (FCC) has been designated by FEMA to manage broadcaster involvement in EAS. The FCC currently provides technical standards and support for EAS, rules for its operation, and enforcement within the broadcasting and cable industries. FEMA works with the emergency response officials who, typically, initiate an EAS message for a state or local emergency. Non-federal EAS operational plans are developed primarily at the state and local level, often with the participation of FEMA and other federal agencies. The FCC provides rules and guidelines for state EAS plans and many, but not all, states have filed FCC-compliant EAS plans. FEMA advisors often help to integrate EAS usage into emergency alert plans. The decentralized process contributes to uneven planning; for example, procedures for initiating a message and activating EAS differ from state to state. In comments filed with the FCC, DHS has proposed that FEMA and DHS "should be the primary point of contact" and act as the "Executive Agent" in managing alerts and warning information. The FCC would continue its regulatory role for broadcasting and wireless communications.[8]

Umbrella organizations that participate in EAS planning and administration include the Media Security and Reliability Council (an FCC Advisory Committee), the Primary Entry Point[9] Advisory Committee, and associations such as the National Association of Broadcasters and state broadcasting associations. States and localities organize Emergency Communications Committees whose members often include representatives from broadcasting companies or local TV and radio stations. These committees agree on the chain-of-command and other procedures for activating an emergency message through radio and television. The constraints of the EAS technology, as specified by the FCC, limit an EAS message to no more than two minutes. Emergency alert agreements with broadcasters, therefore, usually provide for both EAS warning messages and follow-up broadcast programming.

## Broadcaster Participation

The participation of broadcast and cable stations in state and local emergency announcements is voluntary. The FCC has designated over 30 radio stations as National Primary Stations that are required to transmit Presidentially-initiated alerts and messages. Their broadcasts are relayed by Primary Entry Point stations to radio and television stations that rebroadcast the message to other broadcast and cable stations until all stations have been alerted.

The FCC requires broadcast and cable stations to install FCC-certified EAS equipment as a condition of licensing. Radio and television broadcast stations, cable companies and wireless cable companies must participate. Cable companies serving communities of less than 5,000 may be partially exempted from EAS requirements. Direct broadcast satellite companies are among those communications services not required to participate. For the broadcast of non-federal emergency messages, the FCC has ruled that the broadcasters, not a state or local authority, have the final authority to transmit a message.[10] Historically, the level of cooperation from the broadcasting industry has been high. For example, because state and local governments are not required to upgrade to EAS-compatible equipment — and therefore may lack direct access to the technology — broadcasters often volunteer to manage the task of EAS message initiation.

## EAS Technology

EAS technology uses coders and decoders to send data signals recognized as emergency messages. Almost any communications device can be programmed to receive and decode an EAS messages. In manual mode, an EAS alert is sent to a broadcaster, either over an EAS encoder-decoder or by other means, such as a telephone call. Where agreements have been put in place with broadcasters, EAS messages can be created and activated by state or local officials

and transmitted automatically to the public without the intervention of broadcasting staff. These messages use computer-generated voices. All EAS messages carry a unique code which can be matched to codes embedded in transmitting equipment; this authenticates the sender of the EAS message. To facilitate the transmittal of emergency messages, messages are classified by types of events, which also are coded. These event codes speed the recognition and re-transmittal process at broadcast stations. For example, a tornado warning is TOR, evacuation immediate is EVI, a civil emergency message is CEM. When a message is received at the broadcast station, it can be relayed to the public either as a program interruption or, for television, as a "crawl" at the bottom of the TV screen. The installed technology limits messages to two minutes; emergency managers and station operators have pre-scripted message templates that have been timed to fit this constraint; specific information is added to the text at the time of the emergency. When new event codes are added, broadcasters must upgrade their equipment to recognize the codes. To use EAS in a more flexible manner, with messages longer than two minutes, for example, also would require broadcasters to upgrade existing equipment.

## NOAA WEATHER RADIO

Digitized signal technology for EAS is the same as that used for the NOAA Weather Radio (NWR). Widely recognized as the backbone of public warning systems, NWR broadcasts National Weather Service forecasts and all-hazard warnings for natural and man-made events. The compatibility of the signals makes it possible for EAS equipment used by the media to receive and decode NWR messages automatically. Special weather radios are tuned directly to NWR channels. Many can be programmed to receive only specific types of messages — for example, civil emergency — and for specific locations, using Special Area Message Encoding (SAME).

Weather radios can sound an alarm or set off a flashing light. Similar technology is available to provide NWR messages by satellite TV and over the Internet as messages or as e-mail. Technically, the special weather radios available to the public to receive NWR alerts can also receive any EAS message. In reality, broadcast and cable stations rarely program their EAS technology to transmit voluntary state or local messages over the NWR channels. NOAA has improved, and continues to upgrade, its technology to support an all-hazard warning system. It is encouraging public safety officials to notify them as well as their EAS broadcast contacts regarding non-weather-related emergencies so that they may be rebroadcast on NWR. The eventual inclusion of warnings and alerts from the Department of Homeland Security will bolster these efforts.

## ALL-HAZARD WARNING TECHNOLOGY

Given the advanced state of other  communications technologies, especially the Internet and wireless devices, the reliance on delivering EAS warnings by radio and television broadcasting seems out-of-date. Some states and communities are pioneering alert systems that utilize other infrastructures. In particular, many communities participate in programs with e-mail or Internet alerts and some issue mass alerts by telephone. Among the best developed of these warning programs are those used for Amber Alerts, providing noteworthy examples of public-private partnerships. Recently, for example, more than15 states reportedly have launched or are preparing to launch Internet technology customized for Amber Alerts. It is hoped by its developers that this system might become the backbone for an expanded all-hazards warning system that would extend the reach of emergency alerts to all types of communications media.[11]

### Call Centers

Some of the technological solutions for disseminating alerts and providing information rely on call centers, including 911 emergency call centers (also referred to as Public Safety Answering Points, or PSAPs). *The 9/11 Commission Report*[12] describes the often inadequate response of 911 call centers serving New York City.[13] The report's analysis of the 911 response recommends: "In planning for future disasters, it is important to integrate those taking 911 calls into the emergency response team and to involve them in providing up-to-date information and assistance to the public."[14] Such a solution would require a common infrastructure that would support a number of communications and warning needs. Many recommendations have encouraged the development of greater end-to-end connectivity among all types of emergency services.

## Department of Homeland Security

In June 2004, the National Oceanic and Atmospheric Administration (NOAA) and the Department of Homeland Security's Information Analysis and Infrastructure Protection Directorate signed an agreement that allows DHS to send critical all-hazards alerts and warnings, including those related to terrorism, directly through the NOAA Weather Radio All-Hazards Network. Under the agreement, DHS will develop warning and alert messages that will be sent to NWR for broadcast to radios and other communications devices equipped with SAME technology.[15]

DHS is in the process of exploring ways to develop a comprehensive digital emergency alert system.[16] A pilot to test the implementation of digital technologies and networks is ongoing in the National Capital Region and is being expanded to other locations. The extended pilot is part of the Integrated Public Alert and Warning System (IPAWS). It is a joint effort of FEMA, the Information Analysis and Infrastructure Protection directorate at DHS, and the Association of Public Television Stations (APTS). It is testing digital media — including digital TV — to send emergency alert data over telephone, cable, wireless devices, broadcast media and other networks. If successful, the program will provide the base for a national federal public safety alert and warning system using digital technology.[17] The first phase of the program successfully tested the use of common standards for message formats and interfaces, Common Alerting Protocol (CAP).[18]

Another joint program under the IPAWS umbrella is a pilot with NOAA to test a geo-targeted alert system using "reverse 911." Reverse 911 is a term sometime used to describe any calling system that places calls generated by a public safety call center to a specific audience.

A program component of IPAWS is to improve the robustness of the communications network to Primary Entry Point (PEP) radio stations by switching from dial-up to satellite distribution. The number of PEP broadcast stations is to be expanded to provide satellite communications capability to every state and territory. These steps are meant to assure the survivability of radio broadcast communications in the event of a catastrophic incident.[19]

## Other Technology Initiatives

Among other methods being tested to expand broadcast capabilities for emergency alerts are equipping cell phones with NOAA Weather Radio receivers[20] and developing datacasting for digital broadcasting. Datacasting is a one-way broadcast transmission using Internet Protocols.[21] The broadcasts can carry voice and data, including videos, graphics, and text messages. In the D.C.-area Digital Alert Emergency System pilot mentioned above, datacasting is being broadcast to digital televisions and antennae linked to computer networks or directly to computers and laptops. Some advanced wireless phones and other portable devices can receive digital TV broadcasts, as is being demonstrated in several pilots. Satellite radio could also become part of the new era of digital signal alert systems. XM Satellite Radio will broadcast emergency alerts to the D.C. region through a link with the alert system of Arlington County, Virginia.[22] The Arlington Alert network is operated by Roam Secure, Inc, a company that provides text message alert systems to corporations and some governments, including Arlington and Fairfax Counties in Virginia and the District of Columbia. XM Satellite Radio is also a participant in the IPAWS Digital Emergency Alert System pilot.

## PROPOSALS AND PROGRESS

Advocates of all-hazard warning systems are seeking interoperability among warning systems, standardized terminology, and operating procedures in order to provide emergency alerts and information that reach the right people, in a timely manner, in a way that is meaningful and understood by all. In 1999, FEMA and the Departments of Commerce and Agriculture took the lead in a multi-agency working group to explore ways to create an all-hazard warning network.[23] Their recommendations included using NWR as the backbone for a national all-hazard warning system and the establishment of a permanent group to promote improvements in warning systems. The following year, the National Science and Technology Council at the White House sponsored a report that explored the types of technologies and systems that are used or could be used for emergency alerts.[24] Among its recommendations were: the creation of a public-private partnership that would bring all stakeholders together; one or more working groups to address issues such as terminology, technology, location-specific identifiers and cost-effective warning systems; system standardization; and increasing the number of communications channels for warnings. The report concluded that substantial improvements in early warning systems could be achieved through coordination and better use of existing technologies.

Also in 2000, a public-private, multi-disciplinary group was organized as the Partnership for Public Warning (PPW). In 2002, the group received funding[25] to convene meetings and prepare comments regarding the Homeland Security Advisory System (HSAS). Workshop findings were later expanded into recommendations in "A National Strategy for Integrated Public Warning Policy and Capability." The purpose of the document was to "develop a national vision and goals" for improving all-hazard warning systems at the federal, state and local levels. PPW suggested that the Department of Homeland Security (DHS) take the lead in developing a national public warning capability. The PPW discussed the role of an alert system in public safety and homeland security and concluded that current procedures are "ineffective." PPW's recommendations centered on developing multiple, redundant systems using various technologies with common standards that would be "backward compatible" with EAS (including Amber Alert codes) and National Weather Service technologies.

In June 2004, PPW published an overview of emergency alert and warning systems.[26] It subsequently scaled back its activities for lack of funding.[27] The FCC, however, acting on recommendations from PPW and the Media Security and Reliability Council, has issued a Notice of Proposed Rulemaking concerning EAS, seeking comment on how EAS can be improved.[28] The department of Homeland Security is advancing in the testing and probable nationwide deployment of a multi-media alert and warning system using digital technology as part of its Integrated Public Alert and Warning System (IPAWS) program, discussed above.

## RECENT LEGISLATION

The Intelligence Reform and Terrorism Prevention Act (P.L. 108-458) has requirements for a study about the use of telecommunications networks as part of an all-hazards warning system. The study is to be led by the Secretary of Homeland Security, in consultation with other Federal agencies, as appropriate, and participants in the telecommunications industry. Its goals are to consider the practicality of establishing a telecommunications-based warning system that would also provide information to individuals on safety measures that might be taken in response to the warning. The legislative proposal specifies that technologies to consider would be "telephone, wireless communications, and other existing communications networks..."[29] The act also requires a pilot study using technology now being used for an Amber Alert network, to improve public warning systems regarding threats to homeland security. This is to be conducted by the Secretary of Homeland Security in consultation with the Attorney General, other federal agencies, the National Association of State Chief Information Officers, and other stakeholders in public safety systems.[30] According to testimony, FEMA is seeking to finalize an agreement with NASCIO to incorporate an Amber Alert web portal pilot into other, broader-based pilots. These pilots are being coordinated through FEMA's Office of National Security Coordination as part of the IPAWS program.[31]

## EMERGENCY ALERTS AND THE 109TH CONGRESS

There are at least three parts to a warning system: 1) detection of a problem and the communication of the danger to a warning system; 2) dissemination of the warning through communications networks; and 3) information about actions to take in response to the warning or in the aftermath of disaster. In a natural disaster where there is good predictive capability, such as a hurricane, emergency alerts work fairly well. In a man-made disaster, such as a terrorist attack or a chemical spill, the current warning systems in the United States are vulnerable to failure. Too often, the warning is not communicated to any alert system. Communications with people most in need of information and assistance after a disaster is constrained by inadequate systems and often complicated by damage to communications infrastructure. Due to insufficient planning and preparation, there is often confusion about responsibility, priorities, and needed actions. Some observers have noted that the most effective emergency alerts would be able to empower the "first" first responders, those on the site of the disaster when it occurs. Many have emphasized the need for better oversight and planning for an all-hazard warning system. Experts in public safety and communications have observed that it is both possible and desirable to coordinate the development of information networking technology for various types of emergency responses, maximizing the reach of any warning or alert.

## Tsunami Warnings

The horrific devastation across the Indian Ocean from the tsunami of December 26, 2004 raised the level of awareness to the need for better systems for detection and warning, as well as the associated steps for preparedness and response. The Administration has announced plans to expand the U.S. tsunami detection and warning capabilities as a contribution of the Global Earth Observation System of Systems, or GEOSS — the international effort to develop a comprehensive, sustained and integrated Earth observation system. The plan commits a total of $37.5 million over the next two years.[32]   Congressional bills that have measures to improve all-hazard warning systems in the United States include S. 50 (Senator Inouye) and H.R. 396 (Representative Menendez). These two bills provide different perspectives on emergency alert planning, activation and response but they both recognize the need for aggressively advancing the development and deployment of warning systems. S. 34 (Senator Lieberman) would strengthen tsunami detection and warning systems worldwide but focuses on detection and communications among authorities and does not include provisions specifically for improving emergency alerts to the general populace.

### *S. 50*

The Tsunami Preparedness Act (Senator Inouye) builds on the Administration's plan for an improved tsunami monitoring system. Additionally, the bill would improve federal coordination and would establish a task force of representatives of federal agencies, coastal states and territories.[33]  The bill directs the Administrator of NOAA to maximize the effectiveness of detection and warning systems for U.S. coastal communities and to take actions to assist other countries in achieving similar goals. The main purposes of the bill are[34]

- Improve tsunami detection, forecast, warnings, notification, preparedness, and mitigation.
- Extend coverage of existing Pacific Tsunami Warning System to include other vulnerable areas such as the Caribbean, Atlantic Coast and the Gulf of Mexico.
- Increase efforts to improve forecasting, preparedness, mitigation, response and recovery, including education and outreach.
- Provide technical and other assistance to international efforts.

- Improve federal, state, and international coordination for tsunami and other coastal hazard warnings and preparedness.

System components covered in the bill include a number of provisions for detection and information sharing and require a communications infrastructure to alert communities vulnerable to the occurrence of a tsunami.[35] Program components include outreach, education, preparedness and risk management.[36] The bill authorizes a tsunami research program that includes communications technology.[37] The NOAA Administrator, in consultation with the Assistant Secretary of Commerce for Communications and Information[38] and the Federal Communications Commission, is to investigate the potential for improved communications systems for hazard warning networks.[39]   Technologies mentioned include telephones, cell phones and other wireless devices, satellite communications, the Internet, automated alerts on television and radio, and technologies that might be suitable for reaching remote areas at a low cost. Provisions for assistance on a global level include technical assistance to international organizations in developing a global tsunami warning system.   Also, the NOAA Administrator is to give priority in assisting vulnerable areas with needs such as planning, obtaining detection and reporting equipment, and establishing communications and warning units.[40]   To achieve the various goals set forth in the bill, the Tsunami Preparedness Act authorizes $35 million annually beginning with FY2006, through 2012.[41]

## *H.R. 396*

The Early Warning and Rapid Notification Act (Representative Menendez) provides for the establishment of U.S. programs lead primarily by the Department of State and the United States Agency for International Development
(USAID),[42] to give technological and financial support to foreign countries for the development of all-hazard warning systems, and to strengthen existing lines of communication for the dissemination of information on disasters.[43]   The bill centers on early warning systems, the work of organizations such as the International Early Warning Program,[44] and the contributions of USAID to international detection and warning programs.   The Secretary of State is to lead a study that would evaluate the effectiveness of existing communications links and ways to improve them.[45]   The bill provides for assistance, through the Department of State and USAID, for international programs that enhance effective public warning systems.[46]   The bill would also expand the scope of American

research on public warning systems by providing for sharing results, where appropriate, with the international community.[47] Specifically, it would broaden the scope of the Study Regarding Nationwide Emergency Notification System and the Pilot Study to Move Warning Systems Into the Modern Digital Age — required by the Intelligence Reform and Terrorism Prevention Act — to include a component for evaluating the applicability of various alert technologies to other countries.[48] The Secretary of State, cooperating with the Department of Homeland Security, the Federal Communications Commission and the Assistant Secretary of Commerce for Communications and Information (Administrator of the National Telecommunications and Information Administration), among others, is to lead these research activities.[49] Other responsibilities involve the study of evolving technologies that could be used in providing all-hazard warnings in the United States and abroad.[50] The named agencies are also to study the role of satellites, wireless technology and radio frequency assignments in providing emergency alerts, working with the World Radio Conference[51] and other international forums.[52] Authorizations for appropriations to cover the programs would be $10 million for each fiscal year from 2006 though 2010.

### *Tsunami Detection*

The Global Tsunami Detection and Warning System Act (S. 34, Senator Lieberman) deals almost exclusively with provisions for improving detection of tsunamis and the earthquakes that generate them. Programs that would include identifying deficiencies in existing systems worldwide, increasing the number of sensors for detecting tsunamis, and improving predictive capabilities and communications infrastructure would be the responsibility of the Secretary of Commerce, working with the Secretaries of State and of the Interior, where appropriate.[53] The bill provides the sense of Congress that the President of the United States should convene an international conference on global tsunami detection and warning.[54] The Secretary of State, working with the Secretary of Commerce, is to prepare and implement a strategy that would provide for a global network for detection and warning for tsunamis.[55] This strategy is to include a "warning communications system involving telephone, Internet, radio, fax, and other appropriate means to convey warnings as rapidly as possible to all potentially affected nations."[56] Authorizations provide for $30 million for FY2005 and $7.5 million for each FY2006 through 2014.[57]

*Other Bills*

A bill comparable to S. 34 has been submitted in the House (H.R. 499, Representative Shays). Other bills include S. 361 (Senator Snowe); S. 452 (Senator Corzine); H.R. 882 (Representative Boehlert); H.R. 890 (Representative Pallone); H.R. 1584 (Representative Weldon); and H.R. 1674 (Representative Boehlert) — are concerned with tsunami detection and the initial stages of notification.

## Planning for the Future

Shortcomings of public safety warning systems in the United States include

- Limited distribution channels (e.g., EAS uses broadcast and cable, NWR is closely linked to radio).
- Limited interoperability among separately administered networks (e.g., EAS messages provide some commonality but there is no coordination for activating all networks with the same alert).
- Insufficient clarity regarding the responsibility for transmitting alerts.
- Limited flexibility in responding to new types of emergencies.
- Limited ability to identify levels of danger and provide direction for actions to be taken by the general public; there are shortcomings both in the capacity of technology to relay detailed messages and in planning for consistency and coherence.
- Limited reach in distance, in time, and in culturally-aware communications.
- Insufficient solutions to reach the handicapped or impaired.
- Inadequate back-up and redundancy.
- Lack of contingency planning.
- Insufficient ability to define, recognize and contact virtual communities.
- Insufficient attention to the deployment of new technologies and the encouragement of public-private partnerships.

The reports to Congress from the Secretary of Homeland Security and the FCC process of rule-making for EAS will provide additional information for Congress about warning systems and may lead to additional legislative activity.

# OTHER FEDERAL EMERGENCY WARNING SYSTEMS

Federal agencies administer numerous emergency notification systems. Briefly noted below are other warning systems that are used to warn the public and authorities.[58]

## National Warning System (NAWAS)

In 1957, the National Warning System (NAWAS) was established.[59] NAWAS, still in use as an operational warning system, is a dedicated telephone network that FEMA administers and uses to coordinate with national, regional, state, and local emergency management officials.[60] Today the system connects over 22,000 national, regional, state and local emergency management offices. NAWAS disseminates emergency information and instructions.[61]

## Federal Emergency Management System (FEMIS)[62]

FEMIS is an independent network of different communication devices that operate over various media (microwave, fiber optics, and wireline). The U.S. Army installs and operates the system and notifies state and local emergency management officials in the vicinity of chemical and biological weapon stockpiles designated for destruction of accidental, terrorist, or criminal release of the chemical and biological weapon stockpiles. The system provides digital image files of the contaminated geographical area.[63]

## Homeland Security Advisory System (HSAS)

HSAS, the system most recently established in response to the terrorist attacks of September 11, 2001, provides a color coded terrorist attack warning system to federal, state, and local authorities, as well as the public. At this date, Office of Homeland Security (OHS) manages HSAS, with guidance from the U.S. Attorney General. Daily advisories are posted on the Internet, and the Attorney General notifies the federal, state and local authorities of any change to the advisory color code. Public warnings, resulting in a change to the color code, are issued through statements made by the OHS through the media.[64]

## Advanced Weather Information Processing System[65]

AWIPS is a telephone network administered by the Weather Forecast Office (WFO), which is part of NWS. This network is a dial-up telecommunications link, also accessible by an Intranet server, that provides for two-way exchange of severe weather information between the weather tracking and news industry and NWS.[66] This system is used primarily by the NWS to inform the weather tracking and news industry of severe weather, which is then reported to the public through the news media.[67]

## Emergency Managers Weather Information Network (EMWIN)[68]

EMWIN is a satellite communications network operated by NWS. EMWIN broadcasts severe weather information to a commercially marketed 1610mHz radio that provides weather warnings to the public and emergency management officials.[69]

## NOAA Weather Wire Service (NWWS)[70]

NWWS is operated by NWS and transmits severe weather information to mass news disseminators and emergency management officials. The severe weather information is transmitted by weather satellites and then broadcasted to the public via NWR or EAS.[71]

The systems briefly described in Table 1, below, are intended to warn the public, federal officials, state and local authorities, or the weather tracking and news industry, of imminent danger to public health and safety.[72]

**Table 1. Federal Emergency Warning Systems**

| Warning System | Type of Threat | Primary Administering Agency | Warning Recipients | Information Issued | Required Receiving Equipment |
|---|---|---|---|---|---|
| AWIPS[a] | Severe weather | NWS | Weather tracking and news industry | Satellite weather imagery | Satellite antenna receiver |
| EAS[b] | Any emergency | Operated by FCC, administered by FEMA | Public, news media | Voice message detailing information and instructions | AM or FM radio, television, or NWR |
| EMWIN[c] | Severe weather | NWS | Emergency managers, public | Digital message detailing severe weather | 1610mHz radio receiver |
| FEMIS[d] | Chemical and biological weapons designated for destruction contimatination | U.S. Army | State and local emergency managers | Digital image files of contimatinated geographic area | Dedicated computer network |
| HSAS[e] | Terrorist attack | DHS | Public, media, and federal, state and local authorities | Color code characterizing terrorist attack risk and needed protective measures | Internet, news media |

**Table 1 (continued)**

| | | | | |
|---|---|---|---|---|
| NAWAS[f] | Any emergency | FEMA | National, regional, state and local emergency managers | Voice message detailing information and instruction | Dedicated telephone network |
| NWR[g] | Severe weather or any emergency broadcast by EAS | NWS | Public, emergency managers | Voice warnings, watches, forecasts, and advisories | NOAA weather radio |
| NWWS[h] | Severe weather | NWS | Media, emergency managers | Digital images of severe weather | Satellite antenna receiver |

Source: National Science and Technology Council, *Effective Disaster Warnings*, and Department of Homeland Security

a. Advanced Weather Information Processing System
b. Emergency Alert System
c. Emergency Managers Weather Information Network
d. Federal Emergency Managers Information System
e. Homeland Security Advisory System
f. National Warning System
g. National Oceanic and Atmospheric Administration Weather Radio
h. National Oceanic and Atmospheric Administration Weather Wire Service

# ENDNOTES

[1] The National Oceanic and Atmospheric Administration (NOAA) is an agency of the Department of Commerce.

[2] Named after Amber Hagerman, kidnapped and murdered in 1996; also referred to as the AMBER Plan, for America's Missing: Broadcast Emergency Response. Websites with additional information include [http:// www.amberalertnow.org], [http://www.amberalert911.org] and the site of the National Center for Missing and Exploited Children [http://www.ncmec.org]. All sites visited August 8, 2005.

[3] See CRS Report RS21453, Amber Alert Program Technology, by Linda K. Moore. The program and policy issues are discussed in CRS Report RL31655, Missing and Exploited Children: Overview and Policy Concerns, by Edith Cooper.

[4] 911 calls go to Public Safety Answering Points (PSAPs). 211 calls typically go to municipal call centers. The role of call centers in providing warnings and information in emergencies is discussed in CRS Report RL32939, An Emergency Communications Safety Net: Integrating 911 and Other Services.

[5] Final Report of the National Commission on Terrorist Attacks Upon the United States, Official Government Edition, 2004 pp. 286-287; 295; 306.

[6] These recommendations, and others, were affirmed at a Senate Hearing," All-Hazards Alert Systems," Committee on Commerce, Science and Transportation, Subcommittee on Disaster Prevention and Prediction, July 27, 2005.

[7] P.L. 103-337, National Defense Authorization Act for Fiscal Year 1995, Title XXXIV -Civil Defense, Sec. 603 (42 U.S.C. § 5196), amending the Federal Civil Defense Act of 1950 (64 Stat 1245).

[8] Letter dated November 5, 2004 from Michael D. Brown, Under Secretary, Emergency Preparedness and Response, Department of Homeland Security, FCC, EB Docket 04-296.

[9] The Primary Entry Point (PEP) system consists of a nationwide network of broadcast stations connected with government activation points through designated National Primary Stations.

[10] FCC, Report and Order and Further Notice of Proposed Rule Making, Released December 9, 1994, FO Docket Nos. 91-301 and 91-171, 10 FCC Record 1786.

[11] "Signing of 9/11 Bill to Bring the Emergency Warning System into the Digital Age; NASCIO will lead in developing a National All Alert

System." National Association of Chief Information Officers Press Release, January 5, 2005 available at [http://www.nascio.org/press Releases/050104.cfm]. Viewed August 8, 2005.

[12] Final Report of the National Commission on Terrorist Attacks Upon the United States, Official Government Edition, 2004 (referred to as 9/11 Commission Report).

[13] 9/11 Commission Report pp. 286-287, 295, and 306.

[14] Ibid., p. 318.

[15] Department of Homeland Security, Press Room, "Homeland Security Leverages NOAA All-Hazards Network for Alerts and Warnings," June 17, 2004, at [http://www.dhs.gov/ dhspublic/display ?content=3724]. Viewed August 8, 2005.

[16] Testimony of Michael D. Brown, Under Secretary of Homeland Security for Emergency Preparedness and Response, "Federal Emergency Management Agency," House of Representatives, Committee on Appropriations, Subcommittee on Homeland Security, March 9, 2005 and Testimony of Reynold N. Hoover, Director, Office of National Security Coordination, FEMA, Department of Homeland Security, "All-Hazards Alert Systems," Senate Committee on Commerce, Science and Transportation, Subcommittee on Disaster Prevention and Prediction, July 27, 2005.

[17] Testimony of John M. Lawson, President and CEO, Association of Public Television Stations, " Senate Hearing, July 27, 2005.

[18] Information on CAP at [http://www.incident.com/cookbook/index. php/CAP_Fact_Sheet]. Viewed August 11, 2005.

[19] Testimony of Reynold N. Hoover, Director, Office of National Security Coordination, FEMA, Department of Homeland Security, Senate Hearing, July 27, 2005.

[20] Testimony of Christopher Guttman-McCabe, Assistant Vice President, Homeland Security & Regulatory Policy, CTIA-The Wireless Association, Senate Hearing, July 27, 2005.

[21] Testimony of John M. Lawson, Senate Hearing, July 27, 2005.

[22] "Arlington and XM Satellite Radio Partner for Emergency Alert Broadcasts," Government Technology, August 3, 2005.

[23] National Partnership for Reinventing Government, "Saving Lives with an All-Hazard Warning Network," 1999, at [http://www.nws.noaa.gov/ om/all-haz/all-haz1.htm]. Viewed August 8, 2005.

[24] National Science and Technology Council, Working Group on Natural Disaster Information Systems, Subcommittee on Natural Disaster

Reduction, "Effective Disaster Warnings," November 2000 [http://www.sdr.gov/ NDIS_rev_Oct27.pdf]. Viewed August 24, 2005.

[25] Funding came from FEMA, the National Science Foundation, the National Weather Service, the U.S. Geological Survey, and private sources

[26] PPW, "Protecting America's Communities: An Introduction to Public Alert and Warning," June 2004.

[27] Memorandum to PPW Members, June 30, 2004.

[28] FCC, News, August 4, 2004, "Commission Seeks Comment on Rule Changes for the Emergency Alert System," Headlines at [http://www.fcc.gov]. Notice of Proposed Rulemaking, EB Docket No. 04-296, available at the FCC website E-Filing/EDOCS link. Comments can be found by going to the E-Filing/ECFS. In ECFS, click "Search for Filed Comments," insert "04-296" in the box marked "Proceeding," and then search the file.

[29] Study Regarding Nationwide Emergency Notification System, Intelligence Reform and Terrorism Prevention Act, Title VII, Sec. 7403.

[30] Pilot Study to Move Warning Systems Into the Modern Digital Age, Intelligence Reform and Terrorism Prevention Act, Title VII, Sec. 7404.

[31] Testimony of Reynold N. Hoover, Director, Office of National Security Coordination, FEMA, Department of Homeland Security for the Senate Committee on Commerce, Science and Transportation, Subcommittee on Disaster Prevention and Prediction," All-Hazards Alert Systems," July 27, 2005.

[32] Plans for An Improved Tsunami Detection and Warning Systems, Fact Sheet, [http://www.ostp.gov/html/Tsunami FactSheet.pdf], located on NOAA's Tsunami Page at [http://www.tsunami.noaa.gov/]. Both sites viewed August 8, 2005.

[33] From Remarks by Senator Ted Stevens on the introduction of S. 50, Congressional Record for January 24, 2005, published January 25, 2005.

[34] S. 50, Sec. 2. (b).

[35] S. 50, Sec. 3 (b) (3) (F).

[36] S. 50, Sec 4 (c).

[37] S. 50, Sec. 5.

[38] Administrator of National Telecommunications and Information Administration (NTIA).

[39] S. 50, Sec. 5 (b).

[40] S. 50, Sec. 7.

[41] S. 50, Sec. 8.

[42] USAID is an independent federal government agency that receives overall foreign policy guidance from the Secretary of State. It provides economic and humanitarian assistance in over 100 countries [http://www.usaid.gov/].

[43] H.R. 396, Sec. 3.

[44] The International Early Warning Program, which has been planned for two years, is to be created by the United Nations to increase international cooperation in the development of warning systems and related programs.

[45] H.R. 396, Sec. 5 (a).

[46] H.R. 396, Sec. 6 (a).

[47] H.R. 396, Sec. 6 (b) (1).

[48] H.R. 396, Sec. 6 (b) (2).

[49] H.R. 396, Sec. 6 (b).

[50] H.R. 396, Sec. 6 (b) (3). Specific technologies mentioned are "broadcast media, wireline and wireless telephones, other wireless devices, instant messaging via computer , and electronic bulletin boards."

[51] The World Radio Conference is the forum for the negotiation of international agreements that coordinate and enable global telecommunications. It is held under the aegis of the International Telecommunication Union (ITU), a specialized agency of the United Nations.

[52] H.R. 396, Sec. 6 (b) (4).

[53] S. 34, Sec. 2 (a).

[54] S. 34, Sec. 3 (a).

[55] S. 34, Sec. 4 (a).

[56] S. 34, Sec. 4 (a) (7).

[57] S. 34, Sec. 5.

[58] The systems are described in detail in  Effective Disaster Warnings, Report by the Working Group on Natural Disaster Information Systems, Subcommittee on Natural Disaster Reduction, National Science and Technology Council, Committee on Environment and Natural Resources, November 2002 [http://www.fema.gov/pdf/rrr/ndis_rev_oct27.pdf]. Viewed August 8, 2005.

[59] Harry B. Yoshpe, Our Missing Shield: The U.S. Civil Defense Program in Historical Perspective (Washington: Federal Emergency Management Agency, 1981), p. 537.

[60] Effective Disaster Warnings, p. 52.